Praise for DRIVING TO TREBLINKA

'I began to read this book and found the first page so sad I had to put it away until I felt strong enough to face what I was certain—especially given the title—would be a tale of unremitting suffering and sorrow ... Suffering and sorrow there are in abundance in these pages, but the book is not "just" another Holocaust memoir. That said, it may well become—should it find the international readership it deserves—a classic among those books which touch on that atrocity. ... That first page demonstrates the brilliance brought to bear throughout. ... *Driving to Treblinka*, which deals with some of the great themes of 20th-century history, and of one family's history, manages to be both monumental and intimate, and is a remarkable achievement'
— PAUL LITTLE, *North & South*

'Wichtel's prose is exquisite; her wit elegant. She imprints the scale of her longing into the marrow of your bones and I couldn't help but wish to remind her of Siward's epitaph of loss and memory from *Macbeth*: "Your cause of sorrow must not be measured by his worth, for then it hath no end." Some of that worth has already been measured by the tears spilled in unearthing this story, and will be measured again by the tears of the book's readers. Such is the earnestness, the vivacity, and ultimately, the profoundness of its conclusions'
—JAMES ROBINS, *Weekend Herald*

'A searing investigation into family secrets and historic horrors. Several chapters are genuinely distressing to read: not just the descriptions of Holocaust atrocities but also the intimate accounts of how those traumas resonated through the lives of survivors like Ben Wichtel, and then into subsequent generations. ... Yet there's plenty to enjoy. Descriptions of Wichtel's childhood are frequently hilarious ... Wichtel has told the Hitler story again, beautifully, and it is very ugly'
—ADAM DUDDING, *The Sunday Star-Times*

'A stunning memoir ... Wichtel weaves a ... complex, braided narrative that moves forward and backward in time and place ... the book has a gripping detective thread, though what interested me equally, if not more, was the emotional suspense that builds as she confronts family skeletons'
—MARION MCLEOD, *Metro*

'This is a story that reminds readers of the atrocities that ordinary people did to each other, the effect on those who survived, and the reverberations felt through following generations. It breaks your heart, but the side effect of reading this remarkably compassionate approach to an extremely painful history is that it also encourages you to open your own heart, or at least think about doing so. "A book must be the axe for the frozen sea within us," said Franz Kafka. This book is that'
—MARGO WHITE, *The Spinoff*

'Diana Wichtel isn't one to weigh the story down with a lot of unnecessary sentiment. She doesn't need to. Rather than focus on the gloom of her family's history, *Driving to Treblinka* is a brave tribute to the man whose descendants are here because of his actions. It is a story that had me in pieces'
—DIANE MCCARTHY, *Eastern Bay Life*

'I admired the fact Wichtel was willing to share intimate personal details … This is not a book you "enjoy" in the usual sense of that word [but] a salutary reminder of the immense and lasting impact of Nazism. We tend to think mainly of the millions of Jews and others who died in the Holocaust but many of those who survived were, like Ben Wichtel, scarred for life'
—JUDITH MORRELL NATHAN, *Scoop Review of Books*

DRIVING *to* TREBLINKA

A long search for a lost father

DIANA WICHTEL

AWA PRESS

First edition published in 2017 by Awa Press,
Unit 1, Level 3, 11 Vivian Street, Wellington 6011, New Zealand.

Reprinted 2017 (twice), 2018

ISBN 978-1-927249-40-6

Ebook formats
Epub 978-1-927249-47-5
Mobi 978-1-927249-48-2

Cover photograph courtesy of Wichtel Family Collection
Author photograph courtesy of *New Zealand Listener*

Cover design by Keely O'Shannessy
Typesetting by Tina Delceg
Editing by Mary Varnham and Jane Parkin
Map on page 154 by Geographx

This book is typeset in Adobe Caslon
Printed by 1010 Printing Asia Limited

Produced with the assistance of

ARTS COUNCIL OF NEW ZEALAND TOI AOTEAROA

Awa Press is an independent, wholly New Zealand-owned company.
Find more of our award-winning and notable books at awapress.com.

Diana Wichtel is an award-winning journalist, and a feature writer and television critic at leading current affairs magazine the *New Zealand Listener*. After gaining a Master of Arts at the University of Auckland, she tutored English before launching into a career in journalism. She lives in Auckland and was awarded a 2016 Grimshaw Sargeson Fellowship.

For Dad

Contents

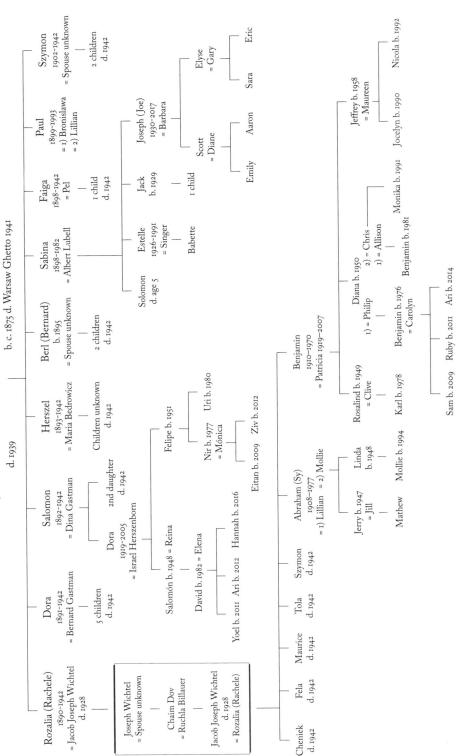

CHAIM JAKOB (YANKEL) JONISZ & BRANDLA FRYDMAN

Author's note

THIS BOOK IS MY PERSONAL ACCOUNT of my father's story. I've tried not to speak for other family members except where they have generously and bravely shared memories, photographs and insights.

For the family members who were murdered in the Holocaust, there are often various versions—Hebrew, Yiddish, Polish—of names. I have mostly used those carried out of Poland in the memory of my great-uncle, Paul Jonisz, and passed on to me by my cousin, Joe Lubell. The birth years, where we have them, are from Paul too, backed up by the few documents that have been found. Many names, most on the Wichtel side, are still missing.

The family tree opposite is meant as a guide only to the relationships mentioned in the book, and as an indication that out of such tragedy some lines carry on. As with so many families with our sort of history, it's a work in progress.

Prologue

1450 GRAMS. I know the weight of my father's brain. 51 ounces, normal for a male.

360 grams. Average size and shape. Ventricles: normal, contracted. Mild to moderate narrowing of the coronary vessels: I know the pathology of a broken heart.

Weight: 165 pounds. Height: 65 inches. 165.1 centimetres. Was he really only 5'5", or had he grown smaller and smaller on his way to disappearing entirely?

Under a heading "External Marks of Violence" is listed ecchymosis on his face. Ecchymosis: a discoloration of the skin resulting from bleeding underneath, typically caused by bruising. Perhaps he had fallen, or maybe, not for the first time, someone had punched him in the face.

The diagnosis of his madness is psychosis caused by arterial sclerosis. He has gallstones. He has emphysema. Cause of death:

1 Acute bronchopneumonia
2 Ecchymoses of right face and eye.

AFTER OUR MOTHER'S BIG CATHOLIC FAMILY spirited her home to New Zealand from Canada with her three children, transported like a clutch of junior convicts, my father wrote increasingly strange letters from Vancouver and from an address in Montreal. Then our mother heard nothing more. That's what we children were told.

Many years later I begin to send letters, emails and begging requests to Canada. Nothing. My brother, living on Prince Edward Island, tries too. All we get are dreary bureaucratic fugues on the same theme: We regret to inform you there is no sign your father ever existed.

I give up, shut the door on the black hole of my family's crazy past into which everything vanishes. I catch myself doubting that the life we lived together in Canada ever really happened. Memory can be a trap. Life wants to go on.

But it is always there, this loss, this mystery that shattered the remains of the Jewish branch of our family, and sometimes still threatens to split asunder what is left of us. For years fragments of a once large Warsaw family have floated free, untethered from each other and our history. The threads that hold us have tugged occasionally. Cousins have made contact, or we have, comparing notes, putting together what we can of a puzzle composed mostly of missing pieces.

One day I talk to my daughter and my niece about the frustration of this search that always leads nowhere. How can you not know where your father is buried? It's absurd, they say. Unacceptable. I've become so habituated to this narrative of gaps and absences that it has almost become normal. "Mum, it's not normal."

Early in 2015 I interview Daniel Mendelsohn, the American classicist, critic, and author of *The Lost: A Search for Six of Six Million*, about his family's Holocaust past. I take the opportunity to get some advice about my own search. "You just have to open the door," he says. "Insert yourself into the stream of history and you'll be amazed what happens. Open the door to the past for good, knowing there's no closing it again."

My brother-in-law, a lawyer, possibly sick of all the kvetching about fruitless quests, does some research on the quiet and offers a lead.

Without much hope I email off my father's details, my birth certificate, and the fee of five dollars Canadian. I realise how many chances I have missed to find out what happened. You miss what you need to miss. For all the obsessing, there had always been a battle between knowing and the thing that might in the end be more bearable: not knowing. You hold on to the narrative you have: my father was meant to come and join us in New Zealand and he didn't. He wrote for a while and then he didn't. Nothing could have been done. End of story. Each time you send off for information about our sort of family you light a fuse and stand clear.

The more I find out the more it dawns on me that all this information, so resistant to being assimilated, will have to be shared with my family. No more secrets and silences. My grandchildren, so safe and trusting in their sunny Kiwi life, will one day know what can happen to a human soul. They may ask how this could have been allowed to happen. How did we let it happen? I think: what have I done?

PART I

CHAPTER I

Daddy Mad Face, Daddy Angel Face

He came to Canada in 1947 ... Port of Entry—Montreal. He made his home in Vancouver where he operated a clothing store.
Clinical record, Brockville Psychiatric Hospital, 1967

"WHO IS THAT?" I ASK.

We're in my parents' room, my mother and I. I'm five or six and studying the photo that sits on my father's bedside table.

"That's your grandmother, Daddy's mother. Her name was Rozalia," my mother says.

"Is she dead?"

"Yes, she died in the war."

"What happened to her?"

"She was killed by the Nazis."

In my memory that's the end of the conversation and I run off to play.

THE HOUSE SEEMED TO DOZE when my father wasn't there. When he came home, it woke up and stood to attention. When I was little I had names for things. There were grey days and good days. There was Daddy Mad Face and Daddy Angel Face. Daddy Angel Face was the one who pulled up in the Studebaker while we were playing in the street late on an endless Vancouver summer's evening, and who enhanced our standing with the neighbourhood kids by producing nickels and dimes from their ears. "Show me a Jew that survives," says a character in Nicole Krauss's novel *A History of Love*, "and I'll show you a magician."

He came bearing chocolate turtles and a whiff of danger. "Punch me in the stomach, hard as you can," he would insist, and laugh as my small fist bounced off muscles trained to withstand blows. He could make a sewing pin sink into his arm by flexing his bicep. "Ben," my mother would wail, "you'll get blood poisoning!" He liked to add a lot of salt to everything, which my mother said would thin his blood. My mother seemed to worry about his blood.

He could make a hole in the end of an egg and suck out the raw contents, which came in handy at Easter. One night when I was four he came home and picked me up and hugged me tight. More often he would scoop me up, set me high on top of the Frigidaire, and wait for me to launch myself into the air, trusting he would always be there to catch me.

He loved to bring home toys and newfangled gadgets: a little bird filled with brightly coloured chemicals that made it perpetually dip its beak to drink; a magic mixer that whipped up a milkshake so frothy it erupted from my mouth and shot across the kitchen when a man came to demonstrate how to use it. We didn't buy one.

We were good at holidays, although not the Jewish ones—except for Passover, when my mother would get out the old mincer that clipped to the edge of the Formica table in our pink and grey kitchen and make gefilte fish, each little ball garnished with a round of carrot. We celebrated Christmas without the Christianity, Thanksgiving without the patriotism.

In those early days there were guests—a stray New Zealander passing through; a new immigrant from the tenement above the store; my father's European friends. There was a feast: turkey; mashed potatoes and candied yams in Mum's best silver chafing dishes warmed by the little candles underneath, all on the white embossed tablecloth I still have. We had a Sputnik ornament on our Christmas tree. "When you grow up, for your holidays you will fly to the moon," my father declared. He promised us the universe. He was in love with the future, then.

At Halloween Mum would carve the pumpkin. With a candle illuminating its wonky jack-o'-lantern leer, it gave off a sickly, slightly sinister smell. One year Dad brought home from his store a tiny man's suit for my older sister Ros, and a prank cigarette that emitted real smoke. I wore a green dress, discreetly padded, and Mum's fox fur. Mum dotted rouge on my cheeks with lipstick and gave me a beauty spot with an eyebrow pencil: we were going for Mae West. Our haul of candy that year was impressive.

My father would buy a pile of lethal fireworks for after the trick-or-treating. He loved setting them off, the bigger the bang the better. The finale was the traditional symbolic act of arson, the Burning Schoolhouse. If I was lucky he let me light it. I didn't like school.

My father worked six days a week: left early, came home late. Sometimes we would go on the bus and visit him at his store, English Textiles. In the front of the shop, all along one wall, were samples of cloth. There was a baroque silver cash register we were allowed to play with—there weren't that many customers—and a changing room. Out back was a workroom with sewing machines and, sometimes, an employee working one. Next door there was a store where you could sit up on chairs that were like red velvet thrones and get a shoeshine. My father would measure up and fit customers, deftly marking with a slab of chalk the material, pinstriped or tweed, already tacked into shape with long even stitches. When he shut the store we would go to his friend's restaurant for clam chowder and then drive home through a city glittering in the dark.

Patricia and Ben Wichtel with Rosalind, two, and Diana, Christmas 1951.

There was always music. My father liked to play his balalaika, which was really just a normal guitar; maybe he had had a balalaika back in Poland. I was impressed by him: his ease with seven languages, his ability to play any musical instrument he picked up. He had a zither and a banjo mandolin. Once he brought home a huge enamelled piano accordion like the ones that wheezed out polkas on *The Lawrence Welk Show*. And always there was the piano. My sister and I were sent to a music teacher up the road, a woman of a certain age whose cleavage loomed over us as she taught. I hated to practise and got to grade three only because, like my father, I was good at learning by ear.

My father playing the piano in his pyjamas on Sunday morning: it was his only day off. There would be singalongs, until we were old enough to rebel. Dad's self-taught style involved sensational swoops up and down the keyboard in the manner of Liberace. Liberace was schmaltzy, my father said, but he liked his show, and Perry Como. His tastes were catholic for a Polish Jew: "Cruising Down The River", "You Are My Sunshine", "When Irish Eyes Are Smiling". He sang "Beautiful Brown Eyes" to me but his clear favourite was "Oh My Papa, To Me You Are So Wonderful", delivered by his daughters with what was probably a disappointing lack of enthusiasm.

There was always "Du, Du Liegst Mir Im Herzen". My mother couldn't understand why he would teach us a German folk song.

"What does it mean?" I asked him.

"You, you are in my heart," he said. "You, you are in my mind."

There were trips to the delicatessen to get lox, matzo and rye bread for Sunday lunch. Afterwards there might be a drive to Stanley Park to feed the squirrels and visit an ancient bad-tempered emu. My father and this bird had a straightforward relationship: he would try to feed it peanuts; it would try to take his hand off. If he was in a particularly good mood he would declare, "The sky is the limit!"—a phrase full of promise of a full-scale blowout on hot dogs, pony rides, plastic windmills and balloons.

My father had brown eyes, a mole on his nose just like mine, and what were considered in our neighbourhood strange continental ways. He would carry a picnic basket on his head, one hand steadying it and the other on his swaying hip, while we screeched with hilarity, and mortification. On one outing he opened a bottle of Coke left too long in our hot Studebaker. It sprayed him full in the face. That was a great day.

My father in the garden: if he was doing chores we were doing chores. In shorts and singlet, he would fire up the lawnmower with its delicious heady smell of petrol. Although he was living a sedentary life by then, he still had the build of a weightlifter.

It was my job to weed the rockery. I hated that rockery. If I was lucky he would let me take a little rod filled with goodness knows what toxic substance and poke the sharp end into the weeds. Garter snakes abandoned their papery skins on the crisply cut lawn, and moles made holes that had to be filled. The Millers next door had a pond with dragonflies and frogs. One winter when the pond froze we tried to skate on it.

He could be funny and playful. For Christmas one year his brother in New York, our Uncle Sy, and his wife Mollie sent my sister and me identical Tiny Tears dolls that cried real tears when you squeezed their tummies after a bottle. My father dandled both babies on his knees, singing a jaunty made-up song: "What a life wiz two granddaughters." There had, he said, been twins in his family.

He had a certain old-world charisma. He would let me do his hair as we sat on the couch watching television or listening to the gramophone. He was my first love. Once, when I was very small, I tried to plant a romantic kiss on his lips—I watched far too many old movies in our darkened basement. He pushed me away, laughing, embarrassed.

He was fastidious: one of the few largely useless practical life skills he passed on was how to cup a toothpick discreetly in your hand at a restaurant. He was always perfectly groomed in a continental fashion: black hair slicked back, white shirts with arm garters to hold his sleeves out of the way when measuring a customer for a suit. Sometimes he would wear a maroon paisley cravat that seemed dashing and then, as I got older, odd and old-fashioned.

We had friends in those days. There was another Mollie, a New Zealand friend of my mother's, her husband Dave, and their daughters Sandra and Debbie. My father called Mollie "a glamour puss" in a not entirely approving way. I was fascinated by her platinum hair and leathery skin—she liked to be tanned. I always knew when the New Zealand Mollie was on the phone by the way my mother said little for an hour but "Mmm … Mmm … Mmmmm."

We had no real family in Vancouver. Mollie and Dave were the closest thing, apart from my father's best friends, who we called Auntie Rose and Uncle Harry. I was a little scared of Rose, who was given to blunt assessments of our weight, dress and manners. At her house the cooking was kosher but she didn't mind eating my mother's Kiwified dishes. Uncle Harry was a lawyer, sweet, legally blind, and always a welcome visitor for his Yiddish-inflected "Donald, Where's Your Troosers?" Once I turned to Auntie Rose at dinner and pronounced, "Daddy says you talk too much." Dad tried to laugh it off. My mother suddenly had the brisket to attend to in the kitchen.

There were pinochle games with Rose's father, Mr Tass, and Harry's brother, Dr Greenberg, our family doctor. Mr Tass was Russian, enigmatic and ancient. Now that it's possible to stalk people online I know he died in 1961 at the age of seventy-two. Dr Greenberg would bring disappointingly healthy treats of liquorice and crystallised ginger. No one ever mentioned the war.

I WOULD GO A LONG WAY to avoid an encounter with Daddy Mad Face. The rage was sudden, out of nowhere: shouting, a fist thumping the table, dishes jumping and no reasoning with him. Once he blamed me and my sister when our brother Jeffrey, then a toddler, knocked himself senseless falling down the back steps of our house.

"But Dad, we were at school," I said.

"It doesn't matter. Stay home from school. Your job is to look after your brother."

I realise now he was terrified something would happen to us.

Our mother never took our side. I remember her standing up to Dad only once. Uncle Leo was Dutch and also not our real uncle. He and his second wife Joanne had a beautiful baby boy who was named Benjamin after my father. When Benjamin was eighteen months old he drowned in a neighbour's pond. The day we were told was the greyest I could remember. Uncle Leo and Auntie Joanne came to our house. As they talked my father said, "If only you had been watching him." I was just six or seven but I knew this was the wrong thing to say. "Ben!" my mother said. "What use is 'if only'?"

My father could change the weather in the house with a word, a look, but he never raised a hand to us; from Mum you'd get a smack in passing if you didn't move fast enough. Once when I was naughty Mum told him to spank me. He couldn't bring himself to do it and we ended up laughing.

In the early years, if we felt like living dangerously, we would court his displeasure by making fun of his accent.

"What's going on in dat house?" he would demand when we played up.

"Which house, Dad?"

"Sit behind the table!" he would order.

"*Behind* the table, Dad?"

I tried to teach him how to say his words properly. "Not 'tousand',

Ben Wichtel with Diana Wichtel (right) and a friend, Kerrisdale, Vancouver, 1958.

Dad. Th… th… th… thousand." It didn't help that we both had a lisp.

In our house, where there were three different accents, language could be slippery. "Mum says she's going to knock our back teeth out," I reported to my father after some transgression. It's the only time I can remember calling on him to defend me from my mother.

"Did you say that to the children?" Dad asked her. Mum indignantly pointed out I'd mixed up two of her maternal storm warnings: "I'm fed up to the back teeth with the both of you" and "I'll knock your blocks off." Dad shrugged. Her New Zealand expressions mystified him.

There was no question of defying my father but it was easy enough to enrage him without meaning to. Once at the lunch table there was a slice left of my mother's meatloaf. As I reached for it my mother said to leave it for Dad. "You're not going to waste it on him, are you?" I wisecracked recklessly. My father exploded, angrier than I'd ever seen him. "How dare you! Get down from the table!" I was banished to the den. I know now he'd heard that sort of thing before—in the other world we didn't speak of. Shop, job, house, food, water, air: don't waste it on a Jew.

I don't know when I first learned that monsters didn't just live in the basement. Apparently they were everywhere and could devour your whole family. There was that photograph beside my father's bed of my Polish grandmother, who had brown eyes and a stubborn curl like mine on her forehead. I don't remember when Dad first told me he had escaped from a train to a death camp, leaving behind his mother, his brothers and sisters Cheniek, Fela, Maurice, Tola, Szymon, and their wives, husbands and children. Maurice was handsome, my father said, and Fela was his favourite sister.

My father and another man had jumped from the moving train. He rolled down a bank in the snow, he said, and lay there waiting to be shot. Somehow the guards didn't shoot. The train moved on and he took off into the forest.

One day he and a companion ran into two young German soldiers in the forest. That should have been the end of them but they pretended to have guns. He demonstrated, putting his hand in his pocket and making a gun shape with his fingers. The German soldiers, just terrified boys, ended up making friends with them and bringing them food.

Most of the time they ate what they could find or steal. They made holes in eggs and sucked out the contents. My sister, a horse lover, remembers my father saying he ate horse meat. They dug up potatoes and devoured them dirt and all.

Rozalia Wichtel (née Jonisz). Born in Warsaw in 1890, she married Jacob Joseph Wichtel and the couple had seven children, including Benjamin, born in 1910.

My father had nightmares. My mother said he would run in his sleep. We knew he had spent a lot of time hiding in a box under the ground. No one told us about the gas chambers, the crematoria, the horrors, but Mum had set herself to read everything she could get her hands on. When I was about eight I made off with her copy of *Exodus* by Leon Uris and read it cover to cover. One of the characters, Dov Landau, is an orphan from the Warsaw Ghetto. He is sent to Auschwitz-Birkenau and forced to join a Sonderkommando, a prisoner work unit made to dispose of bodies from the gas chamber. "He stood

Members of the Wichtel and Jonisz families, from a page in a photograph album. Clockwise from top left: Israel Herszenborn, who married Dora Jonisz after the war; Tola Wichtel; unknown family group, possibly including Brandla Jonisz; Maurice Wichtel; Dora Jonisz.

by until the shrieks of agony and the frantic pounding on the iron doors stopped," I read. "Dov had to go to work with ropes and hooks to untangle the hideous tangle of arms and legs…"

I made up a game to play with my father. When he arrived home late on a cold dark night my sister and I would turn up the collar of his overcoat, muss up his hair, and make him go out the back door again. Cast as a poor homeless wanderer, he would knock at the door and we'd take him by the hand, pull him into the warmth of the kitchen, take his coat, and lead him to the dining-room table, which would be set with hors d'oeuvres of mashed avocado and egg, anchovies, and his single shot of rye whiskey. It was a strangely satisfying ritual I wanted to repeat over and over again.

When I played make-believe games I called myself Fela because she was my father's favourite sister, but after I read about the ropes and hooks and tangled bodies I couldn't be Fela anymore. I no longer tried to imagine what it might have been like for them, for my father, because I couldn't. Think of a panic attack on a plane when you feel you're about to die. Think of feeling that for years, every minute, day and night.

IN HER GRAPHIC NOVEL *I Was a Child of Holocaust Survivors* Bernice Eisenstein writes of a compulsion that came upon her when watching the televised trial of Adolf Eichmann in her basement as a small child in 1961: "Suddenly I'm injected with the white heat rush of a new reality. The Holocaust is a drug and I have entered an opium den, having been given my first taste for free … my parents don't even realize that they are drug dealers."

At eleven I also felt the white heat rush of my father's reality as we watched the Eichmann trial. Eichmann, in a glass bulletproof box: I find myself fighting a sort of pity for this thin balding man, caged and on show, playing with his earphones. But he is the worst human being I have ever seen, a mass murderer. It's here I first hear the word Holocaust. In my memory my mother thinks Eichmann should die. My father does not.

I developed some compulsive rituals to stop the bad things from finding us. On the bus, if my right cheek touched the cold steel pole I had to press my left cheek to it as well or a nameless catastrophe might befall us. Cupboard doors needed to be shut or the clothes and shoes inside would be unhappy. Lollies needed to be consumed in even numbers. (If I'm honest, they still do.) My coat pockets were soggy with abandoned bus tickets I had rescued from winter puddles where they looked sad and cold.

Dad didn't bring home used bus tickets but puppies and kittens and people he rescued. Our spare bedroom was often populated with what my mother called Dad's lame ducks. Peter Weiss, who worked for Boeing, was a regular. I never knew what he was doing there but he taught me to make an omelette and was kind to our cat Goldie. Maybe he was a sort of boarder. There was a glamorous woman called Donné from South America or somewhere, whose elderly mother stayed with us while she had all her teeth pulled out. I walked by the bathroom as she was spitting up gobs of blood, and for years couldn't eat raspberry jelly. Once it was a new immigrant from Poland who was living in the tenement behind his store. Dad asked us to give the man's little girl one of our dolls. I dressed up Rubber Dolly and guiltily handed it over, unable to bear having to choose from the dolls I loved.

By then we had moved to 3389 West 43rd Avenue in the leafy suburb of Kerrisdale, where no one was like us. The house seemed grand, two storeys with mullioned windows upstairs and, in the spare bedroom cupboard, a secret door that led into an attic. There was a backyard with a walnut tree and a cherry tree. Auntie Rose and Uncle Harry came over for cherry-picking parties. The properties across the road ran down to a stream where we were allowed to play, or at least no one stopped us. West 43rd was the house where my father played the piano and we were happy. I still have dreams about houses and they are all enchanted versions of the one in Kerrisdale.

My father, too, had his rituals. Every night he had his one rye whiskey in a small crystal glass, served from a decanter, and his hors d'oeuvres in crystal bowls. He liked things a certain way. He didn't want to answer the phone or a knock at the door. One day we went to Cultus Lake, where our neighbours the Mitchells had a holiday cabin. It was a magic place where you could rent pedal boats, play at the game arcade, and swim. We stayed too long and Dad had to drive home in the dark on the unfamiliar roads. He became more and more frantic. It was our fault for making it happen.

Perhaps he was having bad memories triggered by the trees and the unknown place, panic attacks relieved by shouting at us. Sometimes I asked questions that must have caused him pain.

"How could you leave your mother on the train?"

"They would shoot you."

"Why did you just go? Why didn't you fight?"

"They would shoot you."

"Why didn't everyone run away?"

"They would shoot you."

"How can you be sure they are all really dead?"

"I went back."

For a while he banned us from having toy guns, until we nagged long enough to get Roy Rogers and Dale Evans six-shooters, with caps that gave off an intoxicating whiff of gunpowder. One day he picked up a toy rifle he had bought for my little brother and looked down the sights. "I saw them shoot the breasts off a woman," he remarked casually.

Our wasteful ways enraged him. There was much sitting over congealing plates of porridge. I once carried a hard-boiled egg around in my kindergarten basket until it rotted, rather than admit I hadn't eaten it.

But he was a soft touch. Delegated one morning to take me to kindergarten, he couldn't bring himself to leave me when I clung to him sobbing as the teacher tried to wrench me from his arms. Years later it occurred to me what memories such a scene might have conjured up. He took me home. I could tell my mother wasn't pleased with either of us by the furious way she pulled on her stockings before marching me back again.

He had all sorts of friends: Jewish, German, a Cuban communist called Vic with a beautiful pregnant black wife called Trinny. A neighbour asked Mum how she could let these sorts of people into our house. Mum once mentioned over coffee with some local women that we were going on holiday to Harrison Hot Springs in the Fraser Valley. "Why are you going there?" one said. "That's where all the Jews go."

I knew we were Jewish because Dad was Jewish. When the kids across the road taunted us with boasts that they were related to the royal family, Dad said, "You go and tell them you are related to Moses." We may have been related to Moses but we never went to synagogue, and when Uncle Harry offered to teach Ros and me Hebrew Dad said no. He brought in a young man to teach us French instead.

Later I begged to go to Sunday School like everyone else in the neighbourhood. "My father is Jewish," I happily announced when we were learning by heart the names of the books of the Old Testament. "Maybe your dad could come and talk to the class about being Jewish," the teacher said. I ran home and asked him. "No," he said.

I was so embarrassed by his refusal I never went back.

WHAT DID I KNOW THEN about my father's childhood? I absorbed fragments by the sort of osmosis that conveys information to children in families where there are silences. He was the youngest of seven children. The favourite, he liked to say. In Arabic, Benjamin is Ibn Amin, favoured son of the father; in Hebrew Binyamin, son of the right hand. In the Bible he is the youngest son of Rachel. His mother's name was Rozalia, Rachel in Hebrew.

He almost never spoke Polish, although I begged him to because it sounded funny and singsong and foreign. There was a rhyme that he sang when he bounced a rubber ball, something I could see he was very good at. The rhyme lodged indelibly in my mind so that decades later I would still remember enough to look it up on the internet:

Kipi kasza, kipi groch,
Lepsza kasza niż ten groch,
Bo od grochu boli brzuch,
A od kaszy człowiek zdrów.

It's about boiling grits and boiling peas—peas give you a stomach ache so better stick to the grits, something like that. He never explained it. He seldom explained anything. "Don't ask questions," my mother would say. She worried about upsetting him.

There were tantalising glimpses of his pre-war world. "I would never dare to talk back to my father," he said pointedly. "I would never dare to sit in my father's chair." But it seemed to give him some satisfaction that he'd raised daughters who were less afraid of him. "You are the master of excuses," he would say when I'd learnt to construct elaborate arguments to try to get out of a chore. "You will be a lawyer," he would say, hopefully. Sorry, Dad.

He talked about having to walk miles through snow, praying all the way, to get to school. He was so clever, he said, that he was asked to help teach the other children. There was pride in his voice when he said his father had been a Talmudic scholar. He never said when he stopped believing in the god of Judaism, or in any god.

He talked about his family having to hide at night in a potato field during some sort of pogrom. He was a little boy. Someone stole his blanket.

He wrote to me once in Polish, in my new autograph book, and signed himself, with a flourish, Bronisław. Before that I didn't know he had another name, his Polish name. Bruno for short.

ONE DAY WHEN I WAS NEARLY THIRTEEN I was about to leave school early to go by bus to the orthodontist with my mother, who never learned to drive, when a boy said, "Kennedy has been shot." He had heard it in the staffroom, he said, and some teachers were crying. I didn't believe him—boys had a lot of wrong information—but when we got downtown newspaper vans were prowling the streets with loudhailers and people were ducking into churches to pray. Camelot was over, and I didn't need braces.

By then we were living in Canterbury Crescent, our second to last house, part-way up Grouse Mountain. My little brother called the sparkly night-time view over the city from our picture window "TV Land". For the next two weeks I spent as much time as I could watching the news coverage, which was going on twenty-four hours a day. For once my father didn't say, "Turn off the television. Read a book." I remember the bloodstains on Jackie Kennedy's pink suit, the pillbox hat that somehow stayed on through everything, the look on her face as Lyndon Johnson was sworn in. I had never seen a man shot dead live until two days later Jack Ruby stepped out of the crowd at Dallas police headquarters and murdered Lee Harvey Oswald. It was when I watched this coverage that I felt television's power.

I was haunted for years by the Zapruder footage that showed Jackie crawling with such purpose on to the back of the car. Was she seeking help or trying to escape, planning to jump for her life from the moving car?

My father loved to watch politics and currents affairs, so he and I had been glued to television through earlier international crises too— the failed Bay of Pigs invasion in 1961, the Cuban missile crisis in 1962. There had been air-raid warning drills. People down the road dug up their backyard and built a bomb shelter. My father seemed unbothered but I was terrified. When I left the house to visit my friend Anne I pulled my sweater over my mouth to keep out the nuclear fallout.

The air of impending doom in the world in general seemed to be descending on our family in particular. There were adolescent battles with my father. "Be an individual!" he pronounced. This meant wearing the brown brogues he had bought me, rather than pleading for the fashionable shoes I wanted. When I needed a new dress he took me to the ladies' fashion store of an immigrant friend. The dresses were for middle-aged women. The friend was probably doing him a favour because by then we couldn't afford new clothes.

One morning while my mother was doing the dishes I nagged her about runs in my stockings. She told me I had to just wear them. I kept nagging. She threw a plate on the floor and it smashed with such force that a piece of porcelain flew out and cut the inside of my anklebone, which bled and bled. I was shocked. I'd never seen my mother like that. "What have I done?" she wailed. For years afterwards I would look at my foot and say, "Hmm, you can still see that scar where you threw the plate at me," and she would say, "My own daughter! How could I have done that?"

I know now that she was going under, we were going under, and she was trying to protect us. We were about to move again, to a rented house where we would have to give away the dog and I would be with my father for the last time.

CHAPTER 2

Making it up

Patient married a girl from New Zealand in 1949. They met in Vancouver.
Clinical record, Brockville Psychiatric Hospital, 1967

IN LATER LIFE MY MOTHER would advise against doctors: "They'll only find something wrong with you." She wasn't too sold on looking back either. Old photos made her feel sad.

One story she would tell was how she met Ben. She was on her OE at a time when most Catholic girls her age who weren't in a convent were married and producing children. She had an aunt who had ended up living on Canada's Vancouver Island—the aunt, possibly, who gave her the amethyst brooch I played with when I was ill, which was quite often in those days, when every child got chickenpox, mumps, measles and scarlet fever.

IN 1948 MY MOTHER Patricia Valentina Scantlebury—she was born on Valentine's Day—was pretty, blonde, twenty-nine and single. The oldest child in her family, she had helped to bring up seven siblings, plus her Aunt Alma's three boys. For years she never went anywhere without a toddler trailing behind and never had a bed to herself. That bed was often wet by morning.

During the war she had worked for a tobacco company, W.D. and

Ethel Scantlebury (second from right) with her daughters Rosemary, Patricia, June and Wendy. This photograph was probably taken before Patricia left for Canada in 1948.

H.O. Wills. Her coming-of-age party in 1940 at the family home in Roseneath, Wellington, was approvingly recorded in an *Evening Post* social column, "Here and There", which still exists online. "In the lounges gladioli and coreopsis were artistically arranged." Mum and especially her younger sister Pam were always good at flower arranging. "The guest of honour sang several songs."

Patty and Pam were gadabouts, and pals of Selwyn Toogood, who would become a New Zealand institution as the host of the radio, and later television, show *It's In The Bag*. Pamela Scantlebury is listed as a co-star in Toogood's first screen performance—in drag—in a short film called *Oh! Mr Gadd*. An ad hailed the film as "Wellington's first talkie!"

My mother had stories of trying to be a socialite on slender working-class means. Her dodgy dentistry let her down at a party when a particularly enthusiastic greeting to a friend —"Keith!"—sent a false tooth flying across the dance floor. There was the time the elastic of her handstitched silk French knickers gave way and they fell off as she walked up Lambton Quay. She stepped out of them and kept walking, a survival strategy of stoic forward momentum in the face of adversity that she would maintain.

During the war the girls were enlisted to entertain American soldiers at dances and put on entertainments to welcome young evacuees from the blitz. Nana would offer homesick boys a home-cooked meal and her gruff maternal care. Romance inevitably blossomed. My mother became engaged to an American soldier. After he got appendicitis he was shipped off back to the States and she never heard from him again.

A stint working for the military in New Caledonia produced no new fiancés, and soon she was on the run from a country that suddenly seemed too small. She took almost nothing when she set off from Auckland on board the *Wairata* in 1948. She wasn't to know she wouldn't be coming home.

The passenger list shows Patricia Valentina Scantlebury arrived in San Pedro, California, on March 27. The *Wairata* had sailed from Auckland via "Rapotonga"—Rarotonga. Among others listed as "in transit to Canada" are a minister of religion, an apartment-house owner, and several women whose "Calling or Occupation" is listed as "Home Duties". My mother's is "Steno-clerk". No home duties yet.

In Canada she stayed with her aunt for a while and then went to live in Vancouver city on the mainland, combatting loneliness with slabs of apple pie at a local diner. She got herself a job working for my father at English Textiles, the fabric-importing business his brother Sy had helped set him up in. Almost immediately my father was courting her. In New Zealand she was used to going out with boys whose idea of a good time was to get drunk and vomit out the back of the dance hall. My father would arrive at the door of her rooming

Ben Wichtel with Rosalind, his first child, in the backyard at home in Vancouver, May 1949.

house, elegant in his beautifully tailored English textiles, carrying a bouquet of flowers, kiss her hand, and smartly click his heels in the old-world way.

Soon my father opened a tailoring store, also called English Textiles, at 734 West Pender Street. He and Pat were two people with no desire to look back, washed up in a city where they had no one. Sy and Mollie came up from New York for the registry office wedding; they would later give them an album of wedding photos to mark the occasion. Mum looked lovely in her chic tailored grey suit—no doubt from English Textiles—and a little hat with a fashionable dotted half-veil. My father looked handsome and debonair. My mother told me he had insisted she became pregnant before he would marry her. He was nearly forty and had lost everything. He wasn't messing around.

My sister was born in May 1949. She was named Rosalind Lydia, RL—the initials of her Polish grandmother Rozalia. There are photos of Mum and Dad sitting in garden chairs on the lawn of their first house, receiving guests who have come to see the firstborn. My mother is wearing a satin dressing gown, a hand-me-down from Mollie. In one photo Dad, holding his baby daughter, has an expression of such open-faced joy I almost don't recognise him. They are happy.

Mum was good at making a home under any circumstances. After a few culinary disasters with Depression-era standbys such as creamed tinned salmon and rissoles, which appalled my father, she would master a hybrid cuisine: meat and three vegetables with gefilte fish on the side. Jewish friends came to the rescue with recipes. On a rare occasion when Sy and Mollie made another trip from New York, she cooked a turkey. It was a bit on the dry side but her baked cheesecake with sour cream and crushed pineapple topping saved the day. It helped that Dad couldn't care less about keeping kosher.

I remember my mother mostly in the kitchen and Dad in the living room. They went out together only rarely, once to see a production of *The King and I*. Dad brought home the record and I learned to sing the whole thing. I still can. There was something about Yul Brynner's funny accent, his autocratic ways, and his creative use of the English vernacular—"When I sit, you sit. When I kneel, you kneel. Et cetera, et cetera, et cetera!"—that reminded me of Dad. Deborah Kerr's Anna, attracted to the king, exasperated by him, desperately trying to understand him, reminded me of Mum.

We had little contact with our New Zealand family. Our grandmother Ethel, Ettie to those who dared, sent a book, *The Adventures of Hutu and Kawa*, that featured plump little pōhutukawa fairies. As Hutu and Kawa paddled about in their canoe the worst they had to reckon with was a Fearsome Bush Hawk. We lived in a world of grizzly bears, snakes and other creatures out to kill you.

Four generations of the New Zealand family during 1951 visit by Patricia Wichtel and her daughters. Left to right: Pamela Church (née Scantlebury) with her son James; great-grandmother Annie Murray with Diana; Patricia; Rosalind Wichtel; grandmother Ethel Scantlebury, Ewen Street, Takapuna, Auckland.

I don't recall many photos of my mother's family—maybe they made her feel sad—but there was one of her sister June. My mother was the oldest child in her family and June was next. June was always different. Patty and Pam would arrange dates for her but she yearned for the religious life. The path to it was rocky but June eventually became a nun with the Sisters of Mercy; her religious name was Sister Mary Regis. In the picture her sweet smiling face was elaborately swathed in her nun's wimple.

I was six when June died of cancer. Mum cried. I remember seeing June's last letter to her. She told Mum not to be sad. "I am in the hands of God and I am not afraid." I would sneak into Mum's room to get out the letter and read it. June asked her to bring up her girls in the Catholic faith but this didn't happen. Mum was never religious, although she did allow my sister and me to be baptised when she brought us to New Zealand for a visit, aged two and six months respectively, and her sisters swooped in and carried us off to church.

She was afraid to tell Dad she was bringing two little Catholics back home to Canada but when she finally confessed he said it was okay: we were just girls. When they had a son the boy would be left to him and would not be baptised. I wonder if he would have given Jeff a bar mitzvah.

MY FATHER TOOK TO HIS NEW COUNTRY. He was fascinated with Indian—First Nation—culture. There were Sunday drives to seek out performances, and once he took us to visit an old man he knew who was a chief and lived in a house under a bridge. On these drives into the countryside my father would admire the rugged British Columbia landscape. "Look girls, how majestic!" This would set off a monologue from my mother that I'd hear so often I could chant along: "Oh yes, but it's not as beautiful as the green rolling countryside of New Zealand." My mother was homesick.

When I was eighteen months old and Ros was three, my mother's sister Rosemary came to stay. I have often wondered what Auntie Rosie, then twenty-two, made of our family. After I start searching for my father in earnest, I go to see her in the apartment where she lives with her younger sister, my Aunt Wendy. They've shared a home since they were both widowed. Rosie is one of the few people who remember my parents as a couple.

"Don't hold back," I say over tea and Wendy's cheese scones. I want to know everything.

"I got to know Ben very well," Rosie says. "We had our scraps. He would come home on a Saturday afternoon and say to me, 'Have you mowed the lawns yet?'"

"Was he joking?" I ask.

"No, he meant it. Oh, we used to have fights. He would blow his stack, or I would."

Rosemary Scantlebury visits for Christmas, 1951.

Her language could be a bit choice, she says, "typical Kiwi language".

I ask her how my mother reacted to these scraps. "I don't remember where she was," she says, "probably in the kitchen cooking." Keeping her head down.

My father could be tricky, I say.

"Yes, that's right. I used to think, what the hell are you telling me what to do for?"

She found him a bit strange, she says. "After what he'd been through during the war that wouldn't be surprising."

Did he ever talk to her about what he had experienced?

"No," she says.

She saw the other side of him too, Daddy Angel Face. "He was lovely. We used to have a lot of fun—go out on Sunday drives, picnics, that sort of thing. We played canasta all the time. He loved a game of cards and he loved to win."

He also had a bit of an eye for the ladies, she says.

Flirtatious?

"He was flirtatious, yes." She laughs.

"Did you like him?" I say.

"Of course I did. Yes, I did. He was very likeable," she says.

"Patty wouldn't have married him had he not been," says Wendy, who never met my father. There is fierce loyalty among the Scantlebury siblings.

In those days my father was working long hours at his store in Pender Street. "He was very good to me," Rosie says. "I think he was quite delighted to have me there for a while but then maybe he got a bit jealous. And that's when I thought, oh yes, I'll move on, and I went flatting." Before she went, she tells me, my father offered her a mink coat if she would stay. He didn't want my mother to be lonely.

I ask Rosie if my parents were happy. "They seemed to be very happy, yes," she says. "I think he loved her very much."

While she was working in Vancouver Rosie would pop in for a chat at English Textiles in her lunch hour, or take my father out for coffee. "I can still see him standing outside his shop. Just standing there, smoking a cigarette, watching the world go by."

After Rosie left, my mother's youngest brother Richard, who was in the navy, stayed with us for a few days. After him there were no more visitors from New Zealand.

My father's interactions with my mother's family were minimal. Once he borrowed a home movie camera and we performed awkwardly for a film to be sent to New Zealand. And I remember a conversation with my grandmother on that rare, ruinously expensive and distressing thing, a long-distance phone call. Perhaps it was after June died. "Hello, Muzzer," my father said. It felt sad to hear him say this to a woman at the end of the Earth who he had never met, and in the end never would.

HOW HAD A YOUNG CATHOLIC WOMAN from New Zealand ended up on the other side of the world, married to a Polish Jew ten years older, a man who had survived horrors she would spend a lot of time trying to learn about in her quest to understand him? In my mother's family, too, there was a painful absence that was never spoken of. Secrets and silences roll down the generations like something in the cells that can't be unlearned. When she was five, my mother had been sent to live with her grandmother for a while. Her beloved father, an artist who painted her little pictures, disappeared from her life. At first he sent her a few paintings, then nothing. She became a naughty child, whipped by the nuns at school. She was hurt, angry. Maybe, when she took off to Canada she still was.

I knew a little about Mum's family on her maternal side. Her great-great-uncle, John Joseph Wood, composed the music for the national anthem, "God Defend New Zealand". His friend Thomas Bracken, a poet, wrote the words, strangely passive for a pioneering nation. "God of nations at thy feet / In the bonds of love we meet / Hear our voices we entreat": three lines in and we are already grovelling on the floor, begging for mercy. There's a family story told by my mother's cousin John that it was really Wood's wife Fanny who came up with the tune.

I knew little about Mum's father. I used to say, "You probably have some family out there. We should try to find them."

"No," she would say, "I have enough family."

After she died I discovered that her father, Andrew Pattle Izett, had been both an artist and a journalist. He had married twice, neither time to my grandmother. His mother, my mother's birth grandmother Sarah Izett, was a feminist who ran her own business and was involved in the women's movement and progressive politics. Her birth grandfather James Izett was also a journalist. He had once been horsewhipped outside the Bank of New Zealand in Christchurch after someone took offence at an article he had written in the gossip rag he edited. Mum would have been astonished to know I tracked down a copy of her grandfather's book *Maori Lore* and bought it for ninety dollars.

On my mother's birth certificate her first names are given as Patricia Valentina Pattle and her surname as Murray, like her mother. The first question my aunts asked me when I began digging into my mother's background was whether their mother had been married to Andrew Izett. I had to tell these devout Catholics that when she had her first three daughters my grandmother was living in sin.

June and Pam had both been babies when Andrew Izett left. As far as they knew, their father was William Rymell Scantlebury, known as Scan. June would discover the truth when she first tried to enter the convent. My mother remembered her being sent back home, locking herself in her room and crying. The nuns must have found out about her irregular lineage.

Despite my grandmother's best efforts, the past had caught up with her. By the time I knew her she was an austere presence, with perfectly coiffed hair, blue-rinsed into shades that seemed inspired by the hydrangeas in her garden. She never went to church. Maybe she had dug in her toes after being labelled a sinner and having her children judged. As she got older she would grab my hand as I went by, holding it in a vice-like grip that I understood expressed a desperate affection.

She had a formidable will. My mother told me that when state houses were first introduced she went to sign up for one. By then, along with the three Izett girls, there were five more children with Scan. When things didn't go her way, Nana sat down on the council steps and refused to move until she got a house.

At age eighty-seven and in hospital facing a leg amputation, she turned her face to the wall and died. I had never once, in all the years, heard her speak of my father.

Scan carried on alone in a small flat, where I discovered he could play the piano beautifully. One day my mother discovered his underwear was full of bed bugs. He, too, eventually needed a leg amputated. He took it well. When Mum brought him over from the hospital for dinner, he insisted on unwrapping the stump to show us. He still liked a gin. "The tide's out," he'd say when Mum tried to keep his consumption down. "Don't drown it," when the tonic went in. He was a man of the sea.

My mother encountered her birth father Andrew Izett again only once. When she was eighteen he tracked her down through Auntie Alma, who had a soft spot for him, and asked for a meeting. It wasn't a good experience. "He was just an old balding man I didn't know," she told me. She never spoke a word to her mother about the meeting and never saw him again, preferring to remember with love the father who had doted on her as a small girl, carried her around, and made paintings for her.

CHAPTER 3

In the basement

Patient was always a devoted family man.
Clinical record, Brockville Psychiatric Hospital, 1969

IN FIRST GRADE OUR TEACHER MRS BLINKHORN sent me out of the classroom for talking, then came out and shook me hard. "Are you going to cry or do I have to make you?" she hissed. When we were naughty she spanked us over her knee. Once she said, "Has anyone got a loose tooth?", then made us line up so she could pull out the offending teeth. My mother took all this as normal—she had been whipped by the nuns. We probably didn't tell Dad. He would have got mad.

I avoided going to school when I could and watched television in the basement. Here I could see anything I liked. My favourite was *I Love Lucy*. The early episodes are the work of a comic genius in her prime, and the mismatch of Lucy and Ricky felt familiar. Like Lucy, Mum could be a bit ditzy. Handsome exotic Ricky, his authority often subverted, had a strange accent and was given to blowing his stack. He seemed a sort of Cuban, conga-drum-playing version of my father. I was always looking for my father, even when he was still there.

Most of what I know about anything I learned in this basement. It was marginal territory, a place of liberty and a certain amount of subterranean terror. It was where our pet white mouse disappeared, to be sighted once in the washing basket and then never again. There was a rec room, and a door into the undeveloped badlands where there was a washing machine, and a big black furnace that smelled of oil and the underworld.

There was also a small box of photographs that belonged to my father. In a family with little physical evidence of a history, this was noteworthy. Mostly I remember a lot of snapshots of pretty women. "My girlfriends," Dad would say, a little wistfully. "Cherchez la femme." I asked if any were his dead sisters. He said they weren't but I still liked to scan the faces for resemblances. I always suspected there was more to it.

Incidents that were unaccountable, even by our family's standards, happened in the basement. One day my father came home with a projector and we assembled for a screening of a film called *The Audition*. A lot of young women with huge, scary-looking, barely covered breasts paraded around. They were apparently trying out for some sort of show. I remember Dad saying he had got the film from a friend. According to my mother he was a pushover in business, forever making suits for people who couldn't pay. Perhaps the film was a bizarre form of payment in kind. It swiftly went back to wherever it had come from.

A deck of cards with similarly attired women turned up in our dining room about the same time. It didn't feel right to play *Snap* or *Old Maid* with them. Our friends looked at us oddly. Sometimes I think that my parents, in free fall from their pasts, lacked boundaries.

There were books in the basement. One story, "The Rocking-Horse Winner" by D.H. Lawrence, I read over and over. A beautiful woman has no luck: "She married for love, and the love turned to dust." She raises her children in a house that to her small son Paul forever whispers, "There must be more money!" Driven by the whispers and wanting his mother to be happy, Paul rides his rocking horse frantically and suddenly knows for sure which horses will win at the races. He starts winning and keeps riding until, in a final feverish trance, he picks a derby winner, makes a fortune, and dies of a brain fever.

Our house whispered too. My father must have realised that being beholden to his brother Sy wasn't going to work out in the long term. I remember him saying, "If I only had $100,000." Once, on our annual excursion to the Vancouver fair, Dad parked the car on the way out and ducked in to place a bet at the racetrack. We waited and waited until finally he came out with a win: $200. We celebrated with hamburgers from the White Spot drive-in, delivered to the car on clip-on trays. Dad was happy when he had money in his pocket: the house stopped whispering for a while.

At one point he must have had another windfall because he decided to glamorise the rec room. Workmen came and put in seats with lids where our toys could be tidied away. A bar went in the corner and a red modernist chaise longue arrived. When it was done, my parents threw a New Year's Eve party. There was music, cigarette smoke, the buzz of tipsy conversation. I tasted my first olive out of someone's martini. Afterwards Mum and Dad, unusually merry and affectionate, came and tucked me into bed.

Soon enough the rec room resumed its semi-feral state. The new couch acquired a large perfectly symmetrical hole where a smouldering cigarette butt, dropped by my father when he fell asleep watching television, had drilled down into it. "The house might have burned down," my mother wailed. Having escaped the might of the Third Reich, my father could have died in his sleep on his hopeful red modernist chaise longue.

CHAPTER 4

The bar mitzvah

Two sisters and three brothers were killed during World War II. Patient has one brother living in New Jersey, USA. He is a wealthy businessman who owns a luggage factory.

Dr FS, Brockville, June 15, 1967

"Baruch atah, Adonai / Eloheinu, Melech haolam…"

My father is suffering. He is trying to hold on to a candle and keep it together. His hands, his voice, his whole body is shaking. I am nine and not embarrassed by him, although there are times when I am. The intense foreignness of the occasion and the astonishing sight of my father in a prayer shawl and skullcap—tallit and kippah—have made him seem less like himself and, somehow, more. I've never even seen him wear a hat, let alone a yarmulke, as it's called in Yiddish. I've never seen anybody wear one. We've never been into a synagogue before.

My cousin Jerry is thirteen and now he is a man. This is a very big deal apparently. I haven't seen Uncle Sy and Auntie Mollie since they visited briefly when I was five. We have never met our cousins Jerry and Linda. Vancouver isn't that far from New Jersey but in the fraught geography of our family it has been too far.

The trip to New Jersey has been a long time in the planning. My mother has bought a new outfit, and had her teeth capped and her hair done. Ros and I have had our hair permed and we have new party dresses. My sister's is satiny and eggshell blue. Mine is white and gauzy with embroidered rosebuds on the bodice. I think we look nice.

"They live in a mansion," my father declares. "Wait until you see. They have servants. They will spoil you rotten." He is giving us this gift of this brother who is alive, this brother who is a success.

With a mix, on my part, of wild anticipation and inexplicable dread, we fly to New York. It's my first time on a plane. Jeff, who is about to turn two, won't sit still and is into everything; later my mother will find airline cutlery he has stashed in her flight bag. She doses him with Phenobarbital and eventually he's rendered unconscious on my seat, so I spend the rest of the flight wandering up to the toilet for want of anything else to do.

Auntie Mollie is there to meet us at the airport with her chauffeur. By now, such has been my father's build-up, I'm expecting a New York version of the Queen but Mollie is casual in slacks and odd footwear she calls moon shoes, which she says are very comfortable. She has the distracted air of a woman with the social event of her life to plan.

When we get to the house it is vast, with woodland behind. We walk into the atrium, which has a marble floor—the stage, I will discover, for family dramas that outdo our own.

Sy and Mollie belong to a synagogue. Years later, Jerry's wife Jill will tell me a story. When she and Jerry were high school sweethearts, Sy went to check out her family. The conversation went like this:

—What Temple do you belong to?

—We don't belong to a Temple.

—What do you mean? You have to belong to a Temple to belong to a country club.

—We don't belong to a country club.

—You don't belong to a country club? What do you do?

Jill's parents were socialists.

Mollie and Sy spent a lot of time at their country club: social status was important to them. But even in the 1960s many such clubs were "restricted", mostly unofficially but in some cases blatantly. Up to the early 1970s the Baltimore Country Club had signs that read, less as a warning than a selling point: "No Dogs, No Coloreds, No Jews." In a Groucho Marx story, possibly apocryphal, Marx goes into a club with his daughter, sits down and watches her swim. A man leans over and says, "This club is restricted. Your child will have to get out of the pool." Groucho replies, "She's only half Jewish. Let her stay in up to her waist."

The country club was a privileged man's world. "In the card room there were very serious games going on," Jerry will tell me. "In an afternoon you could make or lose enough money to buy a Cadillac." There were rules. Talk too loud and you got a letter. Walk too fast and you got a letter. "I had portfolios of letters," Jerry says.

Although Dad likes to splash money about when he has it, he is more of a socialist. At Sy and Mollie's house I've fallen down a rabbit hole into a world where everything is out of scale. There is a butler. Ros and I share a room with Linda, who is beautiful and eleven but seems older. Jerry is handsome and very nice to me. It's a place, like in the movies, where children have their own bathroom. They have the first colour television I have ever seen; everyone on it is a futuristic shade of green.

We are given into the care of some sort of handyman, who takes us off with my mother for ice cream. The cone has eight scoops of different flavours. Everything here comes in many flavours.

It soon becomes clear we won't do. My mother is sent to have her hair re-dyed in brown and blonde stripes and Mollie gives her one of her dresses to wear. Ros and I must have new dresses too. We are taken to a fancy shop, where a woman looks at my spherical body and thinks what it needs is a stiffly crinolined cloud of chiffon with

Members of the Wichtel family at Jerry Wichtel's bar mitzvah. Left to right: Jerry, Sy, Diana, Rosalind, Mollie, Ben, Linda, Patricia, Pierre Hotel, New York, 1960.

spaghetti straps. With my gappy front teeth and puppy fat, I look like a chubby chipmunk in a tutu. Rosalind looks grown-up and pretty.

There's a lot of shopping. I'm allowed to choose a toy and select a new type of doll called Barbie. She's wearing a black strapless gown and has a microphone because she is a singer. She also comes with a strapless bathing suit: she is so preposterously proportioned she doesn't need the support. I find her facial features pointy and mean but I am captivated by her clothes, beautifully detailed with tiny buttons and snaps. I will play with her until I'm far too old for dolls. She will travel with me back to Vancouver and eventually on to New Zealand, where my brother and his friend, going through a phase of designing torture methods, will wreck her.

Jerry and Linda have their own bathroom. Linda lets us play with her stuffed animal collection. Jerry shows me his bar mitzvah presents. We have given him a selection of ties from English Textiles. Our ties suddenly seem as wrong as our dresses.

At dinner there is something awful called caviar, which Uncle Sy makes me try. I'm allowed a sip of champagne. I'm beginning to have serious reservations about the tastes of rich people. After dinner we are allowed into the den, a room the size of half our house. Uncle Sy has a stern manner but he lets me play with the crystal chess set.

When we go to the Temple, I'm transfixed by the names, inscribed on the wall, of my dead grandmother and grandfather Jacob and Rozalia, and their children—Dad's and Sy's brothers and sisters Maurice, Cheniek, Szymon, Tola and Fela. Dad has told me these names but I've never seen them written down before.

The bar mitzvah is followed by a ball at one of the fanciest places in New York, the Pierre Hotel, across from Central Park on Fifth Avenue and 61st Street. The hotel, modelled on a French chateau, has the motto: "From this place hope beams." We are driven there in a black limousine. Outside, the city sparkles and hums.

For some reason the ballroom is decorated as a resort with floral beach umbrellas. I spend most of the night alone. Still, I'm allowed to wear lipstick. The older girls jump all over Jerry, perching on his knee and kissing him for the camera. Late in the evening Paul, my father's uncle, sweeps me up and waltzes me around the floor. I recognise him from the photographs of Dad and him in Sweden after the war: he survived too. His dancing style is so frenetic the rough edges of my crinoline rub my skin raw where he grasps my waist. I escape as fast as I can and put on more lipstick.

The photographs of the night present a united family front. In one, Mollie, Sy and my mother sit at a table while Paul and his wife Lillian stand behind. Paul is saying something and Dad is shooting him a sceptical sideways look. In another family shot Auntie Mollie,

Jerry Wichtel and admirers at his bar mitzvah, 1960.

Mollie and Sy Wichtel (sitting, centre) at their son Jerry's bar mitzvah with, from left standing: Paul Jonisz (aka Janiszewski), his wife Lillian, Ben Wichtel; and sitting at right, Patricia Wichtel.

in her strapless white ball gown, is as radiant as a bride. Later she will ask to be buried in this dress. Sy, stylish in his greying crewcut, looks away from the camera. My father and mother have their arms around Linda and the taut suggestion of a smile. Ros looks slender and poised. I look like I'm trying to hide behind her. Jerry, the bar mitzvah boy, fixes the camera with a quizzical challenging gaze. At some point in the evening he will go AWOL, taking off with friends for cocktails at the Copacabana next door.

After the ball we're supposed to stay on for a few days but everything implodes. My brother Jeffrey turns two but there is no party. There is yelling behind the closed door of the library. My father goes home to Vancouver by himself without saying goodbye. We stay on for a day or two, then also leave on the long train journey north. Mollie and

Sy arrange a stateroom, and a suitcase full of games and toys. There's a glass-roofed observation car. My mother has been given money to tip the porters. I leave a trail of fifty-cent pieces wherever I go, happy not to feel the poor relation for a while. At dinner, the lamb chops come with paper frills. I never want to get home.

THERE WAS AN INDELIBLE POWER in the sight of my father looking so alien, so Jewish, so fragile that day at the bar mitzvah. I know now that he was being honoured. As Jerry's only surviving uncle on his father's side, he was given an Aliyah—an ascending to Israel, or in this case to the bimah, the pulpit, to chant a blessing before or after a reading of the Torah. He would have been called by his Hebrew name, Binyamin Ben-Yaacov.

Bless Adonai who is blessed.
Blessed is Adonai who is blessed now and forever.

He was doing a good deed for what was left of his family, fulfilling an obligation. Both brothers were generous when they had the means.

Jerry will later tell me that in the early days Sy would give away a lot of money. When I meet our cousin Joe—who knew Sy as Abraham or Abe—he tells me, "In Yiddish we say Abe Wichtel was a mensch and performed many mitzvahs. He was a true human being and performed many acts of kindness, thereby receiving God's blessing."

But the bar mitzvah marked the peak of his family's fortunes. Five years after this Sy was in financial trouble. Linda and Jerry had to work at his factory when they weren't at school. Jerry had to use his bar mitzvah cash to finish college.

After the bar mitzvah, money still arrived from New Jersey for a time, but Uncle Sy and Auntie Mollie never visited us in Vancouver again.

CHAPTER 5

It's snowing in Vancouver

He is very lonely, and, as you know, without resources of any kind. Have you any news of his wife and children? We wondered if once again you could send him a little pocket money, so he could go to the canteen, or on a little outing during the summer months.

Miss Crawford, social worker, Brockville, June 27, 1968

THE LAST TIME I SPOKE TO MY FATHER I was a bitch.

By the summer of '64 there were tea stains on the ceiling of our house from the times my father would smash the table with his fist in a rage. I was thirteen. One night I was in the upstairs bathroom when he came home and banged on the door, furious, trying to get to his Milk of Magnesia. "I have stomach cancer!"

He was suffering from a few things by then, I would discover, but not that. Maybe it was what his father, Jacob Joseph Wichtel, merchant of Warsaw, had died of in 1928, leaving Rozalia and their seven children to face what he couldn't possibly have foreseen because who could?

My mother would tell me in painful talks years later—I pressing, she crying—that Dr Greenberg had kept ringing her, saying, "You have to get Ben to come into the office." He told her my father was addicted to barbiturate painkillers.

He would shout at her, blame her, belittle her, but still expect sex.

I think she wanted me to have the raw evidence for the defence so as not to blame her for what happened. I would learn from my mother later that by then my father wasn't working in the store anymore after he left the house in the morning. He was sitting in the park feeding the birds.

My father fell asleep every night on the couch. My mother went to bed early. When I'd go into the bedroom to say goodnight she was often crying. For lack of anyone else to confide in—as things got worse he forbade her from contacting their old friends, although sometimes she would sneak out—she confided in me. He wouldn't tell her what was going on. There was no money. What would become of us?

We had a dog that my father had brought home a couple of years earlier, a pure white Alsatian puppy that had been abused. The puppy was frightened of men and cringed when someone approached, especially if they were carrying something. Dad called the dog Duke. I took it as a sign of our family's haplessness when we discovered the dog was in fact female and no one had noticed.

We took to calling her Dukey so as not to confuse her. She remained resolutely untrained, hurling herself at the door when someone knocked, grabbing visitors by the arm. She never actually bit anyone but she looked capable of it. "Where the dog?" became the cry of the bakers and greengrocers who brought produce door-to-door. We would wrestle her into the basement but eventually she learned to turn the door handle and would erupt from the underworld like a hound from hell. In the end the delivery men tooted and waited outside in their vans.

Dukey ate the Barbie doll of the girl next door. She chased cars until a neighbour opened the driver's door in her face. Once, when my father was driving off without her, she ran after the car, sailed through the open driver's window into the back seat, and sat up grinning. Dukey, like everything else, was reeling out of control.

By now we had moved from West 43rd Street in Kerrisdale, the house where we had been happy for almost as long as I could remember, to Canterbury Crescent in a raw suburb of Vancouver's North Shore, a newer cheaper whistle stop on our road to ruination.

One night a man my father knew came to the house. Maybe it was the man who had sold us the house and left some money in, checking on his crumbling investment, or someone with whom Dad was trying to do a business deal. Dukey rushed him, snarling. The man shoved his fist into her mouth and down her throat. Astonished, she sat submissively at his feet. My father never tried to discipline her. Maybe he was soothed by her fierce protective loyalty: he didn't like unexpected knocks at the door either. Each night my mother would give her a piece of toast and honey. Dukey would take it softly in her mouth, pad out to the backyard, and, in some misguided attempt to provide for an uncertain future, bury it.

We children got on with growing up, negotiating the cracks opening up in what was left of our family life. Ros, eighteen months older than me, was asserting her independence. There was no reasoning with our father. An argument over the purchase of a Beatles LP saw her banished to her room for six weeks. After a few nights he brought home a guilty peace offering—Beatles posters for her bedroom wall. The middle child, I learned to keep out of the line of fire. Our home was not a democracy.

My mother, the oldest of eight children in her family, had been made to leave school at fourteen to go to work. She was just grateful her children could read and write. With my father, it was, "You got an A? Why not A plus?" And, "You got A plus? Why not first in the class?"

Comics were forbidden. I kept my stash—*Archie, Little Lulu, The Twilight Zone*—in the back of the wardrobe. One day I was caught in the hallway holding a contraband Beatles album—*Please Please Me*—behind my back as my father engaged me in an unusually lengthy conversation. I stepped away and backed casually into my bedroom as soon as I could. I thought I'd got away with it. When I revisit this memory years later I realise Dad had just been messing with me. The thought makes me smile.

He adored my little brother, eight years younger than me, the long-awaited boy, named Jeffrey Jay after the initials of his grandfather, Jacob Joseph. Mum would tell Jeff he wasn't allowed any more ice cream, one of the select food groups he ate, along with hotdogs and cheese. "We men need to stick together," my father would say with a wink and get him a bowl while my mother fumed. It's the only time I remember my father doing anything in the kitchen. My little brother was turning into a tyrant.

The other families in Canterbury Crescent seemed young, and on the way up. We didn't really fit in. There were new business schemes. My best friend Anne and I were paid to go around the neighbourhood collecting coat-hangers for a dry-cleaning venture that came to nothing. Our house was crumbling. My brother was five when the front yard was dug up to replace a leaking septic tank pipe, leaving an unfilled crater. One of his friends amused himself throwing rocks at the new pipe until it cracked. My father was beside himself, raging on the lawn. Neighbours came out to see what was up. I was mortified that Dad was making such a fuss. I didn't know then that he had no money to fix the pipe. Now it's an absurd metaphor: everything was going to shit.

My mother got some sort of flu and took to her bed for what seemed like weeks. Then she developed dermatitis and Dad made us do the dishes. "Muzzer has sick hands," he said. I found a medical sample container in the car and understood it was a pregnancy test. My mother, then forty-three, fell down the basement stairs and had a miscarriage, a tiny something in the toilet bowl. It was an accident, she told me years later, and a relief. The prospect of another child in her unravelling situation had terrified her.

She went to hospital for a few days. My father had to take care of us. He must have somehow got us dinner. He got mad at me for trying to do the dishes while perched on a kitchen chair, a sit-down protest at having to mind my little brother all day during the school holidays.

As the end approached there were scenes. The house was up for sale. Mum innocently mentioned this to the previous owner. He wanted his money back. Dad was furious. There was shouting. He made her ring Uncle Sy and ask for more money. When, deeply humiliated, she got a refusal he berated her for being spineless enough to beg.

Mum seldom seemed to leave the house. She, who had always seemed so stylish, suddenly looked dishevelled and defeated. They came and took away the piano.

Jeffrey didn't attend kindergarten as we had. We moved to a house in Highland Boulevard, a couple of blocks from Canterbury Crescent and opposite a primary school where he would presumably go when he turned six the following year. He spent his time screaming down our driveway on his bike, across a lethal main road and into the school's entrance. Once he canned and ended up with a lip so swollen he looked like a duck. It felt as though no one was in charge.

We didn't know it yet but Mum was planning her escape.

THE HOUSE IN HIGHLAND BOULEVARD was brand new and rented. It had a square of dirt for a backyard. Dukey's paws and muzzle were always black. One day that last Vancouver summer I was making some Campbell's Crème of Chicken soup in the kitchen when a stranger materialised in the doorway and gave me a fright. Uldis was a twenty-one-year-old student. He was from Estonia and good-looking in a rangy, raw-boned way. He was supposed to be creating a lawn in our backyard. Perhaps we were being allowed to stay in the house rent-free in exchange for doing the garden and my father had delegated the job. It never occurred to me to ask. By that stage there were not many questions to which I wanted to hear the answers.

One night we're sitting watching television. The first documentaries about what is starting to be called the Holocaust are beginning to screen. There is footage of the Warsaw Ghetto, the emaciated bodies, children with haunted eyes in the streets of a civilised European city.

"I was there," my father says. I turn to look at him. His eyes hold steady on the television screen.

"What was it like?"

"You would wake up in the morning and the person next to you is dead."

I don't ask who that person was because you don't ask.

There are images of a place called Auschwitz. "There were worse places," my father says.

I am shocked into silence. I thought I knew at least something about his life until I sat with him and saw those pictures.

I MUST HAVE TOLD THE KIDS at school that we were going to New Zealand before the summer holidays in June because I remember Paul Zaluski saying, "You'll be eaten by the Mau Maus." My mother's family in Auckland sends us copies of *The New Zealand Herald*. I have the ghost of a memory that the newspapers were sent so my father could look for jobs. The television page of the *Herald* reveals one channel that comes on at two in the afternoon and finishes at 10.30 p.m. with a prayer. I flatly refuse to leave, but our life in Vancouver has already ended. In the last two months I stop seeing my friends. We're as good as gone.

The tension in the house is unbearable. I start to get migraines and for the first time go on a diet. Maybe it seems like a plan to try to disappear. The diet is simple: sleep away as much of the day as you can; eat an orange, then nothing else until dinner.

I spend my small window of waking time falling in love with Uldis. We talk about the Beatles. His favourite song is "I Saw Her Standing

There": "She was just seventeen..." He gives me Freud to read. He seems particularly keen on the Id. Our discussions are thrilling. He says something about petting the dog, and, giving me a strange look, adds, "Oh, I shouldn't have said petting." I don't know what he is talking about.

He takes my mother, Ros and me to a movie, *The Incredible Journey*, about a dog and cat who find their way home. We go to a drive-in for a burger and thick shake. I'm so nervous I can't eat. He comes with us when we go to the Pacific National Exhibition. We smile when my father keeps saying, "Everybody stick togezzer" and joke behind his back about roping ourselves together like mountaineers on a dangerous slope. Dad always worries about losing us.

I agree to go with Uldis on the rickety-looking wooden rollercoaster. I learn at thirteen that love will make you do any damn foolish thing. He leads me to the front car. The flimsy little bar that locks into place is totally inadequate. I keep flying forward, hanging on for grim death. He puts his arm across to hold me in.

He teaches me to play his guitar. "Your fingers are so tiny," he says. No one has ever described anything about me as tiny before. Teenagers have just been invented. I model myself on the girls in *Gidget* and *Bachelor Father*, flinging myself on to the furniture in pastel pedal-pushers and arranging my legs in what I hope are attractively nonchalant postures. "Diana is flirting with Uldis," my father announces. Cheeks burning, I beat a retreat.

At night I make Dad his hot milk for his stomach cancer and present it in one of the best glasses, set on a saucer with a folded white serviette. I don't realise how alert we have become to my father's towering presence, mercurial moods and odd Eastern European expectations until Uldis says, "I've never seen three women jump to attention like you do." He is leaving for a summer job as a forestry worker in the interior of British Columbia. The lawn isn't finished. Maybe he's had enough of the tension and the yelling and is jumping off our sinking ship. On his last night my father takes my mother out to a movie, *Tom Jones*. In these bad years this is completely unprecedented. He is trying to court her again, persuading her not to leave. She tells me later that he said to her, "This is my only mistake. Can't you give me a second chance?"

I have agreed to babysit for the people next door, not knowing it's Uldis's last night. I beg my sister to babysit in my place but I have to go. Before I leave Uldis nudges my foot with his guitar, which is lying on the floor, but we never get to say goodbye. The next morning I find a note under my bedroom door. "In case I don't see you again—you are very sweet and wonderful—have fun, be careful and happy." Every day I go to the cupboard under the stairs to strum Uldis's guitar and breathe the pine-cone smell of some work clothes he has left behind.

We have to get rid of Dukey. My mother puts an ad in the paper. A family come in their car with their other dogs to get her. We watch her anxiously staring at us out the back window of their car as they drive away. We weep. My mother, who survived her own chaotic past by not looking back, doesn't think to get the people's contact details. Dad is furious that Dukey has been taken away, destination unknown, and there is no way of finding out her fate. The phone keeps ringing from the ad. My mother can't talk to the callers because she keeps bursting into tears. I have to take the phone and say, "The dog is gone." Dukey, I hope you had a good life.

In these last months my father seems to become greyer, shakier, a nocturnal silent presence. He comes home one night with a gash in his head so bad it requires stitching. He says he walked into the edge of a heavy glass door at the bank. The meeting at the bank can't have gone well.

We begin to spend more time together watching television. No one is bothering to tell me to go to bed so I don't. He likes to watch

Meet the Press. We start to have late night talks about philosophy, politics and religion.

We are living in a conservative Christian neighbourhood. I come home spouting what I have been told at school about Jesus (good) and communism (very, very bad).

"Jesus was a great philosopher," my father says. "He was not the son of God."

And the communists? "They aren't the worst thing in the world."

During these talks I learn to admire his mind. Then I go to say goodnight to my mother. She's crying.

Soon we're packing our suitcases, just what we can carry. Dad is to stay behind and crate up our belongings to send to New Zealand. Even though I am really too old for them I take my Barbie and Ken dolls, my monkey with a plastic banana, and Cubbie, a stuffed toy that Uncle Sy and Auntie Mollie bought me from the Hotel Vancouver. Cubbie, my constant companion, is threadbare from an excess of affection. "Oh, what a nice rat you have," adults say, uncertainly.

My mother packs nothing of any value. The amethyst brooch that was a gift from her aunt, the hand-me-down mink coat Mollie sent from New York, her engagement ring, all have long since been pawned. For some reason she takes a huge hatbox. It won't fit in the planes' overhead lockers and will cause farcical scenes as we get jammed in the aisles.

My goldfish is named Dewey, after my initials DEW. On our last day I carry Dewey, sloshing unhappily in his fish bowl, around to Anne's house. I haven't seen much of her over the summer. We promise we'll write, and do for a while. Recently Anne tracked me down and came to visit me in New Zealand, bringing a new husband who is a former Mountie, and trailing traces of that other world behind the closed door. She couldn't remember much about my father. I begged her to try: there's almost no one left who knew him. Anne did remember something I'd forgotten. One day she and I had decided to write a story together. We were pleased with it and, always on the lookout for ways to get my father's approval, I gave it to him to read. It was about a couple who got a divorce. Why did we write about that? Neither of us knew anyone who was divorced. Anne recalled that my father was not impressed with the theme.

But she hardly ever saw him, she said. I always went to her place, with its Danish Modern furniture and clean-cut blond parents with normal accents, like a family from television. Her mother enrolled us in charm school. Our ship was going down and I was learning the ladylike way to get out of a car.

I can't remember much about the day we left. When we got to the airport I felt a little put out that my father paused to put some fifty-cent pieces into an insurance machine that promised to pay out if we crashed. He always was a bit of a gambler. I don't remember saying goodbye, just turning to wave when we went through the gate. It didn't feel like a big deal: Dad was going to follow us to New Zealand. We would see him soon.

We flew to Toronto in a DC8, then on to Hawai'i, where we stayed a night in a hotel back from the beach in Waikīkī but were allowed to use the pool at the more expensive beachfront section. No one had thought to pack swimsuits so we bought lurid overpriced ones from a beach vendor. After the long flight the ground kept going up and down, as though we were in a lift. Next day we had pancakes for breakfast, then boarded a smaller plane to Fiji, followed by a Fokker Friendship to Auckland's Whenuapai Airport. In that bucketing Fokker Friendship I developed a lifelong fear of flying.

After an eternity we landed and stepped on to the tarmac to a chorus of yoo-hooing from behind the wire fence. In a photo we have my mother looks a little deranged and we girls shell-shocked. I'm clutching the wretched hatbox. The family had clubbed together to finance the rescue mission that had brought us to New Zealand. There was an air of disgrace about the whole enterprise.

We were separated for the convoy home through the damp lush alien landscape. We girls climbed into the back of Uncle Jim's blue Mini. I had never seen a car so small that didn't have pedals. "What do you think of the scenery?" Uncle Jim said. "Lovely!" I quavered, lighting on the correct answer to any question about how we found our new home. "I expected you to be glamorous but you're just ordinary girls," he said. Maybe in New Zealand that was a compliment.

There was a gathering at my grandmother's house to greet us. Other than at funerals, I would never again see so many of our relatives together. My Great-aunt Alma was small and perfectly square. She said "Hooray" when she meant goodbye. Also, "We're a mad lot" and, encouragingly, "It's a great life if you don't weaken."

Four months later it's Christmas. We are living in a tiny prefab beside my grandmother's house, one road back from Milford Beach. My father phones. "Come back, Diana," he says, "it's snowing in Vancouver."

I say, "How can we come back? Mum is working six days a week. We don't even have enough money to buy shoes."

My mother takes the phone away.

I am fourteen, angry, a bitch. He knows how much I love the snow.

PART II

CHAPTER 6

On the beach

*I mis you all terible it is very hard to describe and I only hope I will have
strength enough to carry on until I can see you.*

Letter from my father to my sister, January 1966

MILFORD ON AUCKLAND'S NORTH SHORE IN 1964: bungalows, baches,
tūī, hedgehogs panting through the garden where my grandfather
grows tomatoes, lettuce and silverbeet, and trees that produce strange,
bitter fruit. Even in winter in Auckland you can go barefoot. I kick
a hedgehog by accident, and get a ringworm.

The ice cream is so rich it makes me feel sick. The money is
indecipherable. Threepence can buy a bag of orange squash gums
and milk-bottle lollies. A shilling is a bob, a guinea is a fortune. A
trailer is a caravan. Tea is dinner, but also a cuppa, with everything.
The beach in winter is, like New Zealand, beautiful and empty.

My first letter to Anne, written in transit, had struck a satiric tone.
"Talk about swanky! You should see this jet. All sorts of buttons for
all sorts of things! They even have a separate little air conditioner that
you can adjust to blow a nice little hurricane in your face… We got on
the plane at 9 o'clock and they served a nice little 'snack' consisting of,
and I quote, kebab a la polynisienne, pilau, fruits confites… A couple
of minutes ago a nice stewardess came and served us a nice pineapple

juice. Wasn't that nice? Oh, by the way, guess what I had to drink for dinner? Champagne."

The only sad feelings safe enough to express are about our dog. "We all felt just awful about giving up Dukey. We think she got a good home though because it's a 150-acre farm in Mission and the people know dogs."

We cram into my grandmother's bungalow across the road from Milford Park. I remember the house as greyish-blue, but then everything from those first two years in Milford is tinted grey in my memory. The park looks, as they say here, as though it's been in the wars. There used to be a pirate ship. There used to be a swimming pool with a slide. Word is it's going to be turned into a dolphin pool but for now it's just an empty concrete hole in the ground where rubbish collects.

A photo shows my sister and me, castaways in the shift dresses Auntie Joanne gave us as going-away presents, sitting on swings, smiling wanly into the winter sun. I have expected a version of Hawai'i. Instead I get chilblains, something I've only ever read about in books about English girls sent to sadistic boarding schools.

When everyone has gone home after our welcome afternoon tea, we are left alone with Nana, Grandpa—Mum's stepfather Scan—and Joey the budgie. Joey whistles but doesn't talk, much like Scan. Nana wears tweed skirts, twinsets and hair "set" to within an inch of its life. She has lived a working-class existence bringing up her large family but thinks Keith Holyoake, the conservative National Party prime minister, is a gentleman. My mother tells me that she and any of her siblings who wished to vote Labour had to sneak off and do so in secret. Nana's children adore her. You wouldn't want to cross her.

"Shit!" she says. She's burnt herself getting the tea out of the oven. We three children turn as one, eyes like saucers, to look enquiringly at our mother. We've never heard an adult swear.

Making a salad, Nana discovers the tomatoes that she cut up from the garden have vanished. Scan has accidentally chucked them out with the kitchen scraps. "Silly old fool," she barks, and makes him go out into the night with a torch, crunching snails underfoot, and pick them out of the compost heap.

Nana's place has two bedrooms. Scan and Nana share one. Mum is in the other with Jeffrey, who has an army cot. He has given up his "oing oing", one of a long line of satin-fringed blankets he has stroked to shreds since he was a baby. Jeffrey wants to go home and has to be told we never are.

My sister and I sleep in the sunporch, where we huddle over a one-bar heater. "We wouldn't notice the cold so much except there's no central heating," I write to Anne. "It's just a matter of learning how to hop out of your clothes, into pyjamas, and into bed with a hot-water bottle in the shortest time possible. Rosalind has become very possessive towards the hot-water bottle."

Our family are kind, inviting us over and taking us out, trying to make us feel at home. We have, of course, to go to school and they have to buy everything for us. My uniform for Westlake Girls consists of green blazer and jumper, white blouse, beret "and (don't laugh) 'stretchy grey stockings'", I tell Anne. I don't write about the green serge rompers we wear for sport: they are beyond my powers of description. My classmates roll them up until they look like hotpants. The uniform is rigorously policed via prefects and demerit marks. I start to have nightmares about arriving at school without gloves or the loathed white boater hat.

The culture shock is paralysing. In Canada we wore nylons and kitten heels and makeup. At Westlake we kneel on the gym floor so a teacher can see if our gym frocks breach the not-above-the-knee rule. In Canada there were boys. At Westlake a girl can be suspended for speaking to one on the way home from school.

We're from overseas and therefore assumed to be backward: my mother probably didn't think to bring our school records. My sister started Latin in Canada, so she is put in a good class. I am put in 3 General Academic for the last term, and next year into the even more disreputable 4 General Academic. There's a girl in the class who gets picked up by a police car after school. Some of the others are filling in time until they turn fifteen and can leave by colouring in the noughts on the mimeographed daily notices. The ink on the notices has a delicious heady smell like gasoline.

The first day in 3 General a girl assigned to look after me points out everyone in the class who isn't a virgin. "Do you let boys lie on you?" she says. I try to pretend I know why I would. Our aunts would have preferred us to go to Carmel College, the Catholic girls' school. It's possibly one of them who tells Mum that Westlake has the highest illegitimacy rate on the Shore. Mum stands firm. Her experience of nuns—being strapped at school for doing flips on the railings and showing her knickers—has put her off.

In some ways Westlake is a release from the social anxieties of my Canadian school, where you needed to worry about what you wore and whether a boy would ask you to the Friday night basketball game. But beneath our uniforms' scratchy conformity lurks hormone-fuelled anarchy, a lot of it taking place in the no-man's-land of the bottom field, where boys sneak down from Westlake Boys at lunchtime. The shenanigans are breathlessly related in maths class in the afternoon.

Our science teacher, a stout old trooper who doesn't believe in bras, sometimes takes us to the field to look at nature while she murmurs Tennyson:

All his leaves
Fall'n at length,
Look, he stands,

Trunk and bough
Naked strength.

There are rumours she's a nudist.

In the sixth form, I take German. It's a strange choice, considering. But my father spoke German as well as Polish. When everyone brings their autograph books to school I tear out the message he wrote for me in Polish. I don't want to have to explain who it's written by, or where he is. I mean to keep it but it gets lost.

I know we are destitute. I try to make the most of the situation by casting myself as a girl who finds herself in romantically straitened circumstances, like Jane Eyre ("poor, obscure, plain, and little") or Fanny Price in *Mansfield Park*. My mother is distracting herself by reading her way through the Brontës and Jane Austen, and I am following hard on her heels.

In Canada we had lived in the spiritual vacuum created when a lapsed Catholic marries an atheist Jew. Now religion is everywhere. Our aunts give us lacy black mantillas to cover our heads, and Catholic prayer books with lurid pictures of the Virgin Mary on their plastic covers. We're taken to Mass at Milford's little St Vincent de Paul Church. There's something oddly erotic about submitting to the rituals of veil, holy water and incense, curtseying to the altar, and making the sign of the cross. The beauty of the Latin mass—"Dominus vobiscum / Et cum spiritu tuo"—lodges forever in my mind, like the Hebrew at Jerry's bar mitzvah.

When some relatives return from overseas with a growing number of children, my family babysitting roster increases. I'm fascinated by the ways of this religious household. The living room has a holder for holy water. During Easter the pictures on the wall of the Blessed Virgin and the Bleeding Heart are covered with black cloths. The whole family kneels after dinner on Friday night and says the Rosary.

There's no television and nothing for me to do once the children are asleep but read books about how to tend the dying—"Make sure that a crucifix is placed within their view"—or the lives of the saints, where tortures such as being broken on a wheel are described: "And to make more exquisite her torment..."

For a while I imagine myself as Audrey Hepburn in *The Nun's Story*. I'm trying to make a go of it although I think that all the proper families that surround us at Mass may not always be so perfect. The religious phase soon wears off. The sermons are not in Latin and they sound like a load of rubbish.

At Nana's place there are also rules, unspoken but stringently observed. Mum has warned us never to mention Auntie June. Years later when Mum's other sister Pam dies we know never to mention her name to Nana either. Pam and Nana lived a block apart but rarely saw each other when Pam became ill. It was too painful for them both, my mother thought.

It should be a clue to the way things are going that I also never hear Nana mention my father's name. This is how she deals with things, along with sherry before dinner and, we will learn after she dies, an impressive amount of Valium.

Scan is an inscrutable benign presence pottering about the place. My mother's memories of life after he came on the scene weren't all good, but after watching him work three jobs during the Depression to help raise eight children, three of whom were not his own, she had come to admire him. He is often three sheets to the wind by early evening, having pedalled off on his ancient butcher's bicycle in the afternoon to have a few beers at the Mon Desir. His youngest daughter Jill calls him affectionately "the cycling fool".

One day I'm walking home from school with a couple of classmates when he comes upon us, pedalling erratically and whistling tunelessly, socks tucked into trousers and cap set at an inebriated tilt. My friends laugh: "Who's that old nut?" I keep quiet and watch with mounting horror as he hops off his bike and begins to walk with us. I want the ground to open up, and am ashamed of myself for being ashamed.

In New Zealand they do things differently. "It's impossible to go on a diet," I write to Anne. "You get up and have breakfast, then have morning tea, then lunch, then afternoon tea, then 'tea' or dinner, then a cup of tea before bed." I learn to eat cauliflower with white sauce, steak and kidney pie, and stewed tree tomatoes with cream. Everything is with cream. I'm too scared to say no. But even the spectre of Nana's disapproval won't make me try tripe. And once at Auntie Jill's I see sheeps' brains soaking in pink-tinged water, waiting to be cooked for dinner, and have to tell her I can't eat them.

At night we gather in the lounge with a vague air of formality to watch television. Immediately after dinner it's *Coronation Street*—old ladies in hairnets drinking steadily in a grey and blighted world. Nana loves *The Black and White Minstrels* and shocks me to the core by calling out, "Come on, it's time for the nigger minstrels."

We move into "the flat"—a prefab on Nana's section that she normally lets out. We three children take the one bedroom, while Mum has a single bed by the door. We troop across the lawn to Nana's to watch television.

We're living here when Mum meets Stew. She's working in accounts at Biss Thew Wine and Spirits, popularly known as "Piss and Spew", and he is a dedicated customer. He comes one evening to take her to a movie. He's an airline navigator. He's from Vancouver. What are the odds?

Stew woos us with pound notes, and by cooking a North American treat, pork spare ribs, which he has had a butcher cut up especially. One night Mum rings from Stew's place to say he is "very sick". She has to sleep over to "take care of him".

WE MOVE AGAIN, THIS TIME A FEW BLOCKS AWAY from Nana's to 32 Muritai Road, a bach with dry rot just around the rocks from Thorn Bay. We are living our marginal lives on marginal territory, looking out every day to the surreal symmetry of Rangitoto Island, a sleeping volcano. The first night I can't sleep for the roar of the sea sweeping the ragged edge of our front lawn where the beach begins. We are perched on the edge of the world. Our mother had shown us a map before we came: after New Zealand there is nothing. My father, who loves the beach, always wants to sit as far away from the other people on it as possible. He might like it here.

Around the scrubby patch of lawn at Muritai Road there are arum lilies and hydrangeas but not much else grows in the salt air. The bach belongs to two unseen spinsters, the Gunn sisters. There is a long inventory listing every bent spoon, chipped plate, and weapon in the vermin-fighting arsenal. I've never seen a mousetrap before. Once a seagull falls down the chimney and sits in the fireplace, as stunned to find itself there as we are.

That shack is our first real family home in Auckland. We have two bedrooms. One is for Mum. In the other there are two single beds with faded candlewick bedspreads and, across the bottom, a sort of stretcher for Jeff. The sheets are stiff and the rough army blankets smell of a second-hand shop, or perhaps of the mice we are somehow expected to exterminate. This is our third move in a year.

Next door live my mother's cousin Ian and his wife Doff. I babysit for them too. When Ian and Doff have a gin and tonic in the evening they pour me one. Along the beach a bit is my grandmother's sister, Great-aunt Alma. She and my Great-uncle Les, a lawyer, have a white deco house and three sons, John, Ian and Graeme.

White Christmas lilies grow wild. Nana won't have them in the house because they remind her of funerals. In the backyard my mother hacks ineffectually at waist-high kikuyu grass and Tradescantia fluminensis, a persistent plant known as wandering Jew, with a rusty scythe she has found in the shed. Although she has her job at Biss Thew, because she also has children, no husband and a ropy backstory she is not allowed to rent a house, even a leaky bach, unless the documents are signed by a male relative acting as guarantor. She finds this humiliating but grits her teeth. She is a woman on her own, hacking out a new life for us with a blunt scythe.

Summer at this house seems like endless golden weather. From the beach as the sun goes down you can see the pulsing beam from the lighthouse on the island of Tiritiri Matangi, thirty kilometres north-east across the water. It was built a century before we arrived. In 1965 it emits the power of eleven million candles. It gives me a weird yearning feeling, a lost world across the water, just out of reach. Later I will read F. Scott Fitzgerald's *The Great Gatsby*. Jay Gatsby looks longingly at that green light on the dock across the bay, where Daisy, his lost love, is. His tragedy is the thought the past can be recaptured if you try hard enough. "So we beat on, boats against the current, borne back ceaselessly..." There was a time when my father too believed in a future where the past could be redeemed. "One day you will fly to the moon!"

We are now the children of a solo mother, not that the term is used then: people just change the subject or make up stories. Mine is that our father is joining us from Canada, and as far as I know it's true. Schoolmates keep asking, "When is your father coming?" After a while I don't know what to say.

I am probably depressed. Mum is working six days a week, eight-thirty in the morning to six at night for fifty cents an hour. We are no longer parent and child but flatmates. I get drunk for the first time when she lets us have a bottle of beer on New Year's Eve. A lady from up the road, also husbandless and largely toothless, comes over and drinks gin and tonic. Mum rarely drank in Vancouver; now she lets me start her cigarettes. "The girls", as we are called here, have to shop, cook dinner and look after Jeffrey, who is running wild on the beach. The first time I boil potatoes they turn into a pasty sludge that runs into the sink when I try to drain them. At the Four Square up the road we pick up fish fingers on tick. "Tell your mother she needs to pay her bill," the man behind the counter says one day. "Thirty shillings," he calls after me as I slink away.

Somewhere around this time I devour Nevil Shute's *On the Beach*, about people in Australia waiting to die from the fallout of a nuclear holocaust that has wiped out the rest of the world. They are alone in a beautiful empty landscape where the best available option is to kill yourself.

Writing to Anne is a connection to our lost life. For my fourteenth birthday, my first in New Zealand, she sends me a pair of pettipants, lace-fringed bloomers that ensure modesty under our shorter and shorter skirts. In a letter to her I list my other presents: two pairs of nylons, a bottle of talcum powder, a bracelet, a pendant, a pair of white shorts, a box of toffees "and a bottle of lovely pale pink nail polish (also some money)". Did I get anything from my father? I never mention him. Anne never asks.

My tone is remorselessly chirpy. "Remember those dolphins I wrote about? Talk about a schmoz! They were supposed to have four but so far only one has materialized and they have it all penned up in the smallest part of the pool—around here the dolphin pool is just a joke." We communicate via caricatures of our old maths teacher, Mr Hill: "Here is Elwin drowning … glug, glug, glug." And the Top 40: "Record Corner: 1. A Hard Day's Night. 2. House of the Rising Sun—I didn't like it at first but it kind of grows on you. 3. Blue Beat." In a cruel twist of fate, we had left Vancouver just before the Beatles arrived to play there and landed in New Zealand just after they left. It seemed symbolic.

When it comes to writing about boys I exaggerate my limited success. No one seems to go on dates. When I make a new friend, Adrienne, we just wander around. Cars with boys often pull up. Once, Adrienne hops in. I can't think of how not to so I hop in too. She's in the front with one boy. I'm in the back, frozen with terror. "What's wrong with your friend?" says the boy in the back seat. I flee as soon as I can. The entirety of my mother's advice on sex: "Boys can't control themselves."

She's pretty much given up telling us what to do. "I've told you what's what," she says briskly. "Now it's up to you." I feel burdened by responsibility for myself. I don't want to let her down and our new life is too rocky for any more catastrophes.

Our roles are gradually reversing. Stew goes back to Canada to sort out his affairs—he has a wife, two daughters. Mum doesn't hear from him for a while and ends up weeping like a heartsick teenager as we go for long walks up the beach, me drawing on my vast experience of male–female relationships to advise her. She works so hard. She's been through a lot. I want her to be happy. I just wish that didn't mean Stew.

He's coming back. I know because my mother buys cushions from the second-hand shop and we're not allowed to sit on them. He moves in. Soon my friends are saying, "Oh, so this is your father from Vancouver." Well, no," I say. "Not exactly."

We receive letters from my father, regularly for a while. Many years later I ask my mother what happened to them. She threw them away, she says. Just couldn't handle it.

Once while working on this book I wake up at dawn heartsick. The day before I have been reading the only one of my father's letters we still have. It is to my sister. "There is no moment in my life here without thinking about you," he writes. "I wish I could control it … I mis you all terrible … No kidding it breaks my hart not to able to see you all."

"No kidding." I can hear his voice.

He adds, "Does Jeffrey remember me? Is he ever saying anything about me? I would like to kno."

MY FATHER'S LETTERS START to become strange, irrational. He is sending them to Sy and Mollie's address in New Jersey and they are sending them on. He seems to think we are there, living with them. I see the postmark and don't understand. Dad knows where we are, doesn't he? He saw us off on the plane to New Zealand.

That last letter to my sister comes from Montreal. I don't know why he has gone to Montreal. He doesn't say. Then the letters stop. My father seems to have dropped off the edge of the world. Mum may still be in contact with him: we know she's in touch with Mollie and Sy because a box of hand-me-down clothes arrives from them. I ask her straight, late in her life, whether she was really expecting my father would join us, or had she left him for good? She says that when she left she thought he would come, although by then the prospect frightened her. He must have applied, because she was contacted by the Department of Immigration and asked if she wanted him to come. She swears she said yes. She also tells me that Scan, who had worked for a time as a clerk in a government department, rang someone he knew in Immigration and told them not to let him into the country.

When I'd spoken to my aunts Rosemary and Wendy years after Mum died, I'd asked them what they knew about her decision to come home to New Zealand. "She must have been very distressed, your mother, to have left and come back. I think she probably thought of you girls and Jeff," Wendy said.

"I think she had it really tough but she never spoke about it really," Rosemary said. "She wouldn't have come back to New Zealand lightly."

What was the story the family in New Zealand were told? "What

I remember is that Ben was coming down later. That's all I heard," Rosemary said.

My mother always told me that when she began to learn how sick my father was she looked into going back to Canada, but she had no money. She contacted the Canadian Embassy but it wouldn't help. Her family told her if she went back to him that was it: there would be no more tickets to New Zealand.

In the letter to my sister, which is dated January 1966, my father doesn't mention coming. In that last telephone call, Christmas 1964, he had asked me to come back to Vancouver. I remember wondering why he was saying that when he was coming to New Zealand. You can get so used to nothing making any sense that you stop asking questions.

In my memory the phone call with my father always takes place on the beach, but of course it couldn't have. Now it occurs to me that it might have been made from the phone box by the beach. Maybe my mother didn't want Nana to know she was phoning him. "Call me at Christmas," he may have said. "Let me speak to the children."

WE WERE IN THE BACH ON MILFORD BEACH when the crate just seemed to materialise, an emissary from another dimension, the world that existed now only in dreams, and in letters to Anne. I know it was around March 1965 because I wrote to Anne, typing with many crossings out, "Aren't I clever? We just got a lot of things sent from Vancouver including this typewriter, hence this letter."

There was our glass-topped mahogany coffee table. Why send a coffee table? There was a painting of a vase of roses, in a frame gilded by my mother—she gilded everything she could get her hands on. There was a New Haven ormolu mantel clock with a cherub, and a vase painted with pastoral scenes—my father liked to go to auctions. There was also the crystal decanter and one of the little crystal shot glasses. The heavy stopper of the decanter has since been broken and glued back together. I've never been able to bring myself to use it.

Dad had packed just three volumes of the set of *Encyclopaedia Britannica* he had bought from a door-to-door salesman. Why only three of the twenty-four? I remember my mother mentioning there were supposed to be three crates but only one ever turned up. Perhaps the remaining volumes are mouldering with the rest of our stuff in a warehouse somewhere in Canada.

I still have the painting of the roses. The other three paintings that came in the crate are long gone, including a faux Utrillo street scene that decorated the wall of Ros's and my flat in Mt Eden Road until someone stole it. A startlingly ugly painting of a grim old lady sitting in a chair with her hair pulled back in a bun was quickly dispatched. My mother couldn't stand it; in Vancouver it had been banished it to the rec room. She called it "Whistler's Mother" and thought my father may have bought it because it reminded him of his mother, but in the only picture we have of Rozalia her face is soft and pretty and she is smiling.

Mum rapidly sold the old lady in the chair to a second-hand store in Milford. As I write it occurs to me she must have known by then that Dad wasn't coming to New Zealand. Or maybe he had told her to sell the painting. Not long afterwards I was flicking through a copy of *New Zealand Woman's Weekly* when I saw a photo of our grim lady with a beaming new owner and the headline "Junk Shop Art Find". Mum had got a couple of pounds for it. She was a child of the Depression. You did what you had to do.

Years later, in the '90s, she would flog off another of the paintings, a large landscape of a path through a forest that reminded me of our family outings in Stanley Park. It took me a while to realise it had gone from the wall of the unit in Devonport where she and Stew lived in their old age. I begged her to tell me if she was ever going to get rid of anything else from Vancouver. We would pay her whatever she was offered. I tried not to sound cross but she looked crestfallen and I felt bad.

When parents run from their history, they also obliterate the history of their children. There is a heartbreaking scene in Art Spiegelman's graphic novel *Maus*, an audacious rendering of the story of his father Vladek, a Polish Auschwitz survivor. Art's mother Anja, also a survivor, ultimately killed herself. Art asks his father to find the diaries she wrote about what she went through. Vladek finally admits he burned them after she died: "These papers had too many memories."

My mother, too, needed to make a clean start. She sold my father's paintings, and threw away his letters and the papers that would have told us where he was. But you can't so easily shake off the past. She didn't know that the things she needed to leave behind in order to survive were precisely the things I needed to hang on to.

How can I judge her for this? I wasn't facing up to things either. When I wrote to Anne I said, "We just got a lot of things sent." It took a careful syntactical contortion to avoid saying, "My father sent some of our things." When tragedy was arriving, crated up from Vancouver, I was writing "Record Corner" for March 1965: "Goodnight, Roy Orbison; You've Lost that Loving Feeling, Cilla; I've Fallen in Love with a Snowman, Little Millie Small. We went to see Cilla Black, Freddie and The Dreamers and Sounds Incorporated. ... Dave Clark is coming soon and there are rumours the Beatles are coming back. I sure hope so."

I wasn't going to tell Anne I thought my father had gone mad.

CHAPTER 7

The Girl From Ipanema

I will do my best for you, you can be sure.

Letter from my father, January 8, 1966

BY THE TIME I KNOW MY FATHER is never coming we are living in another tiny cottage, this time in Williamson Avenue, a street back from Takapuna Beach. My mother now has Stew so renting is easy, although life in Takapuna isn't without drama. Mum's sister Pam, married to a doctor, had told Nana to phone my mother and tell her not to rent the house in Williamson Avenue because it was next to some of their wealthy friends. Mum dug her toes in and we moved in anyway.

The falling out is soon forgotten. Nana quite likes Stew: he's loud and he makes her laugh and charms her with a giant ornamental tortoise from one of his exotic destinations. But Mum and Pam don't see much of each other, which Mum is sad about.

In Williamson Avenue, I share the tiny sunporch that is my bedroom with Jeff when he is at home. Now eight, he has been packed off to board at Dilworth School for boys from difficult circumstances, a move organised by Mum's boss at Biss Thew. Mum is told Dilworth will be good for Jeff. When she takes up with Stew and is no longer solo, she has to keep this a secret from the school. De facto boyfriends aren't part of the picture.

Jeff likes the school, which has small classes and some wonderful teachers, but hates boarding. One of the most painful memories from that painful time is our driving him back to Dilworth every other Sunday evening. He is miserable. We are miserable. He is trying to be a brave soldier.

After Stew has been on the scene for a while, Mum tells me he wants to adopt Jeff and change his surname to Downey. "No," I say. "You cannot do that. He is a Wichtel." She also says Stew would like me to call him Dad. "I can't," I say. "I have a father." In the end I call him San, short for Papa-san, as a compromise.

At night Stew's flying buddies cram into our minute living room and drink. Some get a little flirtatious. There's no chance of sleep in the sunporch with Herb Alpert and the Tijuana Brass's "Spanish Flea" on high rotate until the small hours. Stew discovers "The Girl From Ipanema": "DAH-da-da-da DAH-da-da-da-da…" Sometimes the LP is allowed to play to the end. There is blessed silence until the screech of the needle as it is dragged back to the beginning again. To this day I hate that song. Mum and Stew have a squeaky bed, which is more than any fifteen-year-old should have to bear. I lie in my little cot with my pillow over my head, wondering how we have come to this.

Stew has had to give up his job with Air Canada to be with Mum in New Zealand. A sometime Theosophist, he once spent years on a spiritual quest and tries to school us in the sayings of Krishnamurti, including "Happy is the man who is nothing". In reality Stew is obsessed with temporal things. He has painted a mark on the bath showing how much hot water we children are allowed, and decrees we can use only three squares of toilet paper at a time: rules we ignore. I'm touched, though, when he knocks up desks in the sunporch for us out of apple crates and plywood so I can study for School Certificate. And he lets my friend Judith and me drink his favourite fire water, Benedictine, when she is over for dinner.

There's no privacy at Williamson Avenue. If you're in a hurry to answer the phone you run through the house's zigzag geometry, bouncing off the walls. To get to the back door you have to walk through the bathroom. One night when I go to the toilet Stew is lying in the laundry like a cast sheep, tangled up in the ironing board, too drunk to get up. Another evening, when I'm on the phone to Judith, he's bellowing over his after-dinner Benedictine. "They're all a little high here," I tell Judith. Stew hears me and explodes. He storms out of the house and doesn't come back for hours. My mother tells me off for upsetting him, as she used to do when we accidentally set our father off. But Stew's not my father. From that day I begin to plot my escape.

It's at Williamson Avenue in 1968 that Mum finally tells us where Dad is. She and Stew are going to Japan. Stew has burned his bridges with Air New Zealand and Canadian Pacific Airlines with all his comings and goings. He has been offered a job by IATA, the International Air Transport Association, as a navigator for Japan Airlines. The job will be well paid. Despite the domestic disasters that have left both of them with nothing, Mum and Stew will be able to buy a house when they come back to Auckland.

It seems Mum has to be married to Stew if she is to accompany him to Japan. It's this predicament that forces her to finally tell us Dad is in a mental hospital in Ontario. She has made contact with the hospital to ask my father for a divorce. The hospital has said he is in no state to have papers served on him.

I understand from this that my father is now so ill he is beyond reach. I am eighteen. The age of majority in Canada is twenty-one. If I had contacted his doctors would they have refused to tell me anything? My mother was afraid to reopen the door to the chaos of the past: she had more immediate chaos to deal with, flying off to Japan with the semi-alcoholic, slightly unhinged man from Canada

Stew Downey, Patricia Wichtel and Jeffrey Wichtel, Nikko, Japan c. 1969.

who was not my father. But she should have said we could still write to him and I should have tried.

Mum and Stew spring Jeff from Dilworth and take him to Japan. He has no chance to say goodbye to his teachers and friends. "They basically kidnapped me," he remembers, "picked me up for the May holidays and I never went back. Every once in a while in Dilworth you would see a boy who was leaving and it would always be the same: he would drive away with the new dad. Off they'd go, like in a fairy tale. Suddenly I was one. I didn't know anything about Japan but I didn't care. Stew was my saviour."

AFTER MUM TOLD US WHERE DAD WAS I no longer felt anger, just a low constant thrum of pain. There are things you have to live with all your life that will wake you at dawn. In his last letter he had said to my sister, "I very seldom remember dreams but last knight you were sitting beside my bed and when I opened my [eyes] I looked all over the room to find you. I don't want to drametize but it seems to tragic that after so many years together I can only reach you through this piece of paper."

Then he addressed me: "Diana I worrie about you a lot I don't know why, maybe because you seldom write to me. If you can spare a few minutes for a short letter I would greatly appreciate."

I've read that letter dozens of times. Now for the first time I hear the reproach in his words. "If you can spare a few minutes for a short letter..." I cling to that word "seldom". I must have written to him.

Then he seems to recall the last time we spoke on the phone, when I told him Mum was working six days a week and we had no money for shoes. "I feel sad when I think of mother that after all these years she has to work at the moment. I will try as soon as possible to send some money I am having my tees fixed and it cost a lot of money." It's th-th-th teeth, Dad.

I've made him feel bad for not providing for us. "I will do my best for you," he promises, "you can be sure."

Remembering is an exercise in self-loathing. Later I will talk about these things in New Jersey with my cousin Jerry and his wife Jill, and Jill will say, "You were a child. You didn't have a vote." In Manhattan my cousin Linda will say, "He wouldn't want you to feel guilty. You were a thirteen-year-old girl, what could you do?" She will add of her father Sy's drinking: "Even as a thirty-year-old I couldn't do anything. Could I have kept him from going down that path? No, I couldn't and I was here. You cannot feel guilt, you've got to stop. You have to work on it. You have to work hard."

Linda has worked hard on confronting our family's past. She will tell me, "If you go deep inside—this sounds really crazy—but if you go deep inside yourself and you remember that man, the nice moments you had together and the love he had for you, you can bring that back anytime. It's not gone."

I'm working on it. During one of my random internet trawls of our family names I unearth a piece by a University of Maryland academic about transmitted trauma. The professor has read online an essay I wrote about my father and the game I made up to play with him, in which he was a homeless man at the door and my sister and I brought him in from the cold. He sees this as an acting-out of my father's Holocaust experience.

"We neglect the degree to which the child and adolescent needs to know and feel the inner reality of the parent, even if this reality includes horror. Without this access, everything feels phony, unreal, including the child him or herself. If the parent has been horrified, then the child needs to be horrified too if they are to be securely attached.

"He and his children seem to have been able to play-act his duality, his frightening strangeness that was also a closeness, in a way that worked to contain the horror. Had this part not been shared, the young girl would have been less attached, not only to her father but to life itself.

"There are many ways to interpret her story," the professor concludes. "One is that her father gave her a great gift."

In the game I was trying to ask my father about the past he couldn't talk about and he was trying to share it. While I'm grappling with this I have two vivid dreams. In one I'm in a high room. Perhaps it's the Sargeson Fellowship room in Albert Park, where I have worked on this book. My father is there. For some reason, we have to get out of the room. "You have to jump from the window," he says. "No, it's too high," I plead. "You have to go down there and catch me." In the end we run down the stairs together. In my haste to get down I knock into him and he nearly falls.

In the other dream my father is sitting beside me. He reaches out and takes my hand. I ask him, "Is it okay that I'm telling your story?"

After these dreams, as with earlier ones in which I see my father in a crowd or on a bus, I wake flooded with relief, electrified by love. Some people would say my father has visited me. I wish I could believe this but I'm my father's daughter so I can't. But maybe in remembering him fully and giving in to the pain, he's at the door again and I have invited him in.

I hope that when I read his last letter I wrote back.

CHAPTER 8

A call in the night

His condition is very precarious.
Clinical record, Brockville Psychiatric Hospital, November 26, 1970

SUMMER 1971. The phone rings and rings. At two a.m. it's never good news. Uncle Sy and Auntie Mollie are calling from New Jersey. My sister and I stand in the hallway of the old villa near the corner of Dominion Road and Balmoral Road where we are flatting and learn that our father is dead.

How did they get our number? We're students, living a nomadic life and not in the phone book. We don't think to ask. Maybe they have already spoken to our mother in Yokohama but that's unlikely: my sister remembers that Sy and Mollie were shocked to learn from us that Mum was in Japan and we were in New Zealand fending for ourselves.

What do I remember about the call? Almost nothing. I was numb, stunned. Mollie and Sy gave us their phone number. We lost it. Everything to do with my father ended up getting lost, or thrown out. Just as his presence used to sizzle through the house like an unearthed electric current, reminders of him had a dangerous wattage. The shaky equilibrium of our new life required the door to the old one stay closed.

"He died a few months ago," Sy said. "It was pneumonia. All he left were a few papers."

I didn't ask why we hadn't heard sooner. Now I know that Sy had gone bankrupt; he and Mollie had had to move from their mansion and were no longer in contact with my father. No one was in contact with my father. I will find a document that states: "Family could not be reached." It took a while for the authorities to track his brother down.

At the end of the call Sy says to me, "Never forget you are a Wichtel."

Why didn't I think to ask for the papers about Dad's death? Why weren't they sent to us? Mum may have said she didn't want them, those reproachful postcards from her painful past. Later, when I begin looking for my father, I ask my cousins Jerry and Linda if they saw any of the papers in their parents' effects. They didn't. Maybe Sy couldn't bear to keep them, either.

It seems incomprehensible that we didn't even think to ask Sy for the name of the place where our father died. We could have written, made calls, found out what had happened to him. It will be over forty years before I write the letters and make the calls. "The living are more demanding." Primo Levi wrote. "The dead can wait."

WE PHONE MUM. She doesn't say she will get on a plane and come to New Zealand and I don't ask her to. The next night I go to bed and cry for hours. That is it: no cards, no flowers, no condolences. I don't recall any of my mother's family mentioning this turn of events. In that respect my father's death was like that of his family in Poland: it left no trace.

There is only an oblique reference to the death in my mother's letters from Japan: "Next time you write would you also send me the address of Mollie and Sy. I can't remember the house number, don't even know if they are in the same place. I would like to write them.

Have you written them yet? We really should keep in touch with them I suppose as they were very good to us. I'm a coward I suppose but I hate the thought of opening up the past again."

"Of course we won't forget you. What a thing to say," she writes in reply to what must have been a reproachful letter from me.

I find something else in the letters. A year earlier, a ghost from our old life has passed through Auckland. "Imagine seeing Dr Greenberg," my mother writes. Dr Greenberg had been our family doctor, the one who said, "You have to make Ben come into the office." One of those who tried to help him.

"Life is strange isn't it," she continues. "Am looking forward to seeing them here. I suppose he was amazed I was living in Japan. Yes, it would bring back poignant memories which I'm not looking forward to."

My mother's letters show how much she wants my sister and me to come and live with her in Yokohama. Stew can get us there for free on Japan Airlines while we are still students. "For cripes sake don't worry about money!" he writes. I don't even consider going. I fled home at seventeen, moved into a flat, and have been supporting myself ever since. I am doing a BA at Auckland University. There's no turning back.

NEVER FORGET YOU ARE A WICHTEL, Uncle Sy had said. The name has been nothing but trouble. Just before I left home I went to a pub—the Victoria Hotel—with my best friend Judith so she could meet a boy. She told her parents we were going to the movies; I was the alibi. I was seventeen. The legal drinking age was twenty-one. I ordered vodka, the only drink I could think of. I stood clutching the glass, radiating guilt.

A cop made a beeline and marched me outside.

"What is your surname?" he said, pen poised over notepad.

"Wichtel," I said.

"Do you expect me to believe that? Your mother's maiden name?" he sneered.

"Scantlebury," I sighed. I was going down.

Judith and Johnny came out to try and help. "It's okay, we know her."

"Well, what's her name then?"

Certain I wouldn't have been stupid enough to give my real name, they could only say, "Ahh… we don't know."

I got on the bus alone and cried all the way back to Takapuna. The cop rang next day and asked to speak to a parent. Luckily my mother was still around. He was astonished to find the phone number I had given was real, that I'd been idiotic enough to tell the truth, and that one family could have two such improbable names. He must have thought this was punishment enough because that was the end of my brush with the law.

In reality my mother had amassed enough names to pass for an international secret agent: Patricia Valentina Pattle Murray Izett Scantlebury Wichtel Downey. There was an excess of names on my father's side too. Many of his family had both Hebrew and Polish names. My grandmother was Rozalia and Rachele, my father Benjamin and Bronisław. We knew my father's only remaining brother as Sy but on official documents he is Abraham Szlama Wichtel.

I gave up my name when I got married in the '70s but, despite the endless bother it causes me, claimed it back when my husband and I split. W-i-c-h-t-e-l: I learnt early to automatically spell it out. Over the years, I've had letters addressed to Witchell, Wincell, Mitchell, Twitchell, and Wotchpell. During my life as a television critic I've had hate mail addressed to almost every anagrammatic permutation and vengeful pun, including "you stupid Bitchtel". One plus: when a reader writes in to berate me for a minor error I am almost always able to reply, "Thank you for the feedback, and by the way my name, which you have spelt incorrectly, is Wichtel."

ONE YEAR IN THE LATE '60s, before I know my father is dead, I move flats nine times. My boyfriend Philip and I live in abject poverty. I clothe myself in vintage men's white dress shirts and mouldering fur coats from op shops. There are epic parties, with bands and light shows. Someone has a wind-up gramophone. Entertainment is doing the Charleston around the lounge to a 78 of "The Varsity Drag". Some of our flatmates are classical musicians so we eat crumpets in the overgrown garden serenaded by violin and oboe. The toilet is also in the garden. To wash our clothes we boil up an old copper in the shed.

Parents are best avoided. A flatmate's mother is appalled when she opens a bathroom door and finds the bath piled with dirty dishes we've hidden for her visit. "My son cannot live like this!" she says to me accusingly. As the only female present, I am clearly responsible for the comfort of her layabout boy.

There are, of course, drugs. I'm usually the timorous one—reality is rocky enough. We know people who die of overdoses but my friends aren't in that dangerous league. It's less *Easy Rider*, more *The Young Ones*. One Sunday afternoon there is a motorbike convoy to Titirangi, where someone has spotted masses of dope growing wild. I hate this kind of expedition, always fearful of being caught and having to go through the names again, but too scared of being judged straight and boring to refuse to go. The boys stuff pillowcases with the illicit greenery. Back at the flat they spread the windfall on the roof of the laundry shed to dry: highs for all; fortunes to be made.

It turns out to be catnip. When it comes to grand moneymaking plans, my hippie surrogate family seems as hapless as my real one. The only substance-related emergency is when two of our rock musician flatmates put what they think is sugar in their tea, not noticing the bag is labelled "borax". We take them to hospital and listen to them vomit.

Fortunately it's 1969 and no one needs to grow up. There are Jumping Sundays in Albert Park: agitprop theatre and dancing in fairy rings to the Frank E Evans Lunchtime Entertainment Band, which plays revolutionary numbers like "If You Knew Suzie" and "I've Never Seen A Straight Banana". Led by Tim Shadbolt, we are against nuclear bombs and the war in Vietnam, but mostly we are united by a sense we are living in a ridiculous little country. Women can't go into most public bars, the movie of James Joyce's *Ulysses* can be seen only in gender-segregated audiences. When I refuse to stand for "God Save The Queen", an old woman pokes me with her umbrella.

BEING STATELESS, HOMELESS, FATHERLESS can be a lifestyle choice. I wasn't alone in starting from scratch. I developed an obsession with the Bloomsbury Group. Virginia Woolf and Vanessa Bell—orphaned, siblings lost along the way, living always in the shadow of madness and death, had somehow created a new family, their own world. "Arrange whatever pieces come your way," Woolf had written. Out of nothing, something.

Philip started various companies with names like Cerebral Vortex. That one may have been the poster-printing business. The posters were printed in Brown's Mill in Durham Street, and he schlepped them around the country in a Hillman Imp that kept breaking down.

Decades later a guy would come up to me at a media event and say, "Nerve Centre Light Works" and I would make a spectacle of myself by screaming involuntarily. This was a business Philip set up to create psychedelic light shows. Baking soda, food colouring and oil were smeared between glass slides and the slides put into a projector. The heat would produce kaleidoscopic, pulsating, amoeba-like shapes that, depending on what you'd ingested, more or less blew your mind. I learned to help out and we worked at events involving bands like Ron and Alistair Riddell's Original Sun.

There were anarchic entertainments organised by the university arts society: medieval banquets, complete with straw on the floor, dogs, and on one infamous occasion a stripper. Caterina De Nave, who would later clear the way for women in the television industry, rode around on a motor scooter decorated with a daisy and projected movies on the wall of the Student Union building. Alan Brunton, soon to create the experimental theatre troupe Red Mole, read poetry to jazz. We once visited the grim house in Boyle Crescent where the poet James K. Baxter lived but he wasn't at home. All the bedrooms had locks on their doors.

There were Hiroshima Day events and demonstrations against the Vietnam War but the world seemed largely absurd. I had an ingrained mistrust, possibly inherited from my father, of rigid ideology. Mao and Stalin could not be my heroes: any country that wouldn't let you leave was a prison camp. The world seemed best explained by Samuel Beckett's *Waiting for Godot*. When Vladimir said, "To all mankind they were addressed, those cries for help still ringing in our ears!" and Pozzo says, "They give birth astride of a grave, the light gleams an instant, then it's night once more" I understood that Beckett knew something about the Shoah.

Mostly, though, I had no connection with anything Jewish, although I gravitated to pockets of continental culture. Our group haunt was Babel, a coffee shop upstairs in Victoria Street run by an immigrant, Odo Strewe. Odo had fled Nazi Germany but we never talked about that.

I SOMEHOW FINISH MY DEGREE but don't bother with the graduation ceremony: for years afterwards I will not be able to bring myself to go near the university, afraid I will die of nostalgia. Philip and I are thinking, for practical reasons, of getting married. At Christmas I go to Yokohama to visit Mum and Stew. Our family are the only foreigners in their neighbourhood. No one speaks English. Babies cry at the sight of my mother with her blonde hair. The air is so polluted we blow black stuff out of our noses after walking outside. I smoke, cry, can't breathe. Beset by insecurity I wait for mail that takes weeks to come. I have a small breakdown and imagine that the ramshackle existence back in Auckland, by then the only sense of home I have, will be gone by the time I return.

When I get back in February 1970, Philip is still there. We move to a flat in Balmoral Road and are living there when my mother and Jeff come to stay. Mum and Stew are planning to return, and Mum is looking for a house on the North Shore. I am anxious in case Nana finds out I am living with my boyfriend. "It's not really any business of the family what you do, but as you say it's best not to upset Nana at this stage," my mother has written. "However we will deal with that when the time comes, if it is necessary."

Next year Philip and I take off to Europe after Stew gets me a free ticket from Japan Airlines. We work in London temping as telephonists, jobs that come with a crash course in Britain's class system. At a West End law firm I am told off by a partner for not giving him his messages as he passes by: he doesn't seem to notice I am not the woman who usually sits there. Later, when he sees a man in a turban delivering something, he goes to his office and rings the switchboard. "Are you all right?" he says pointedly. I assure him I can cope. I am from New Zealand.

My next job is at Westminster Social Services, where no one seems shocked to see a mother and children who have been sleeping rough all night. A man who phones isn't happy with the person I put him through to. He knows where I work, he yells, and will be waiting. At the end of work days I stick my head out the door, scan the horizon and run for the tube station.

For a while we stay with Philip's mother, who is working as housekeeper for a newly rich family and has a flat in the basement of their flash townhouse. She doesn't get on with the wife. "Provincial slut," she mutters, referring to the woman's home management standards rather than her morals. Philip's mother is one of the few people who acknowledges my Jewish heritage. "She's a real New York Jewess," she will say of some friend. "You will know what I mean, Diana."

Philip and I take off to Amsterdam, buy a Kombi van that leaks oil, and drive around Western Europe. Once, on a train, we meet a couple of men from Poland. I tell them my father came from Warsaw. I don't say he was Jewish. "Oh, Poland is beautiful. You must go there," they say. That seems a mad idea. We stay in Europe for a few months but I am homesick for a home I don't really have.

Back in Auckland in 1972 we get married. I take a job as a teacher and we move into Philip's parents' home, a sort of elegant 1950s shed in Devonport's Glen Road. His father is living in Canada. His mother comes back from London and sometimes lives downstairs.

Glen Road never feels like home. In truth, my life never feels like my life until I have my first baby, in 1976, in a little maternity hospital in Auckland's East Coast Bays. In those days you stayed in the hospital for ten days. Babies are kept in a glass-fronted nursery and brought to you for feeding. I elbow aside my visitors so I can gaze at my son through the window. My mother, who's said she'd brain the first one of us to make her a grandmother, is broadsided by emotion. "I didn't know it would be like this," she keeps saying. Neither did I. I am twenty-six and can't even take care of myself. I call the baby Benjamin after my father.

I go back to university, get an MA in English and tutor. Life opens up. I am too busy to think often of the past, but armed with a beautiful boy with the Wichtel build who sees no obstacle he can't climb, it seems closer. I am getting ready to start looking for my father.

First, though, I find Chris. I have begun going to encounter groups on Waiheke Island run by Marvin, an American who's trained with the Esalen Institute in California. It is 1981 but on Waiheke it is forever the '70s. My first weekend group is a motley crew: we look like escapees from a Diane Arbus photograph. On an outing to Palm Beach I run into a colleague from the university English department and find myself at a loss to explain what I'm doing.

The disappearance of my father comes up when it's my turn to try and figure out what's wrong with me, but the story feels remote, as if it happened in some other world to some other father and daughter. I make no connection between what happened to our family and my panic attacks, anxiety and hopeless passivity.

I don't learn much in the group other than to make exaggeratedly intense eye contact when I greet people, something that startles my colleagues in the staffroom, but I go back to Waiheke, this time for a week. The co-leader of this second group is Chris, an architect and school teacher. Chris barely speaks to me, which makes me so nervous I constantly bludge cigarettes from him. For days we smoke together in charged silence. One day he asks if he can join me on the sofa. I say yes and scoot over to make room. "No, like this," he says, and lies down with his head on my lap.

He is twenty-six, I am thirty-one. We are both rockily married and both have a son called Ben. Chris's father is an Anglican priest. His mother died of cancer when he was thirteen. He'd been sent away to school camp and never got to say goodbye to her. In his family, too, there are silences. He knows his mother was born in Damascus under mysterious circumstances, and was raised in Israel. He will later find out that during the war she worked in British intelligence. Like my father she spoke several languages, including Hebrew and Arabic.

There are reasons, barely grasped at the time, why people are drawn to each other. I wonder what my father would have made of my new relationship. I think he and Chris would have understood each other. By accident I have ended up with a nice Jewish boy.

CHAPTER 9

A brief history of shouting at the newspaper

Anti-Semitism died the day the victors of World War II opened the Nazi death camps.

Columnist, *The New Zealand Herald*, 2004

WHEN MY DAUGHTER WAS EIGHT her class talked about the Holocaust. Her hand shot up. "Half my mother's family were killed by the Nazis," she announced. She learned early the meaning of the expression "conversation-stopper".

Monika was born when I was forty, into an atmosphere of greater openness about our family's history. By then a picture of my father stood on my dressing table. Chris had digitally extracted him from an old family photo in an album Dad had sent from Vancouver, had the image framed, and given it to me as a birthday present. I sent copies to my sister and brother. Jeff didn't say much about it but his wife, Maureen, told me he put it by his bed.

I had been circling and gradually closing in on my father. It was like a game I had found thrilling as a child. In *Mother, May I?* players advance in increments on the "mother", who, with her back turned, randomly dictates the progress—two baby steps forward, one giant step back—until you catch her. Even when I was taking a step back from thinking about the past there was always a hum of low-level engagement, a secret pleasure when people said, "Oh, you're such a Jewish mother", a kinder way of calling me a Woody Allen-grade neurotic. My children just called me paranoid—"Yeah, yeah, the Nazis are coming to get us, Mum" and "Not everything is about the Holocaust"—although when I instructed them to feel around and pull out all the wires to attract attention should they ever find themselves locked in a car boot, my information came less from reading about the Nazis and more from watching Oprah.

There was a tentative step forward in 1993, when my sister told me about the Auckland Second Generation Group for children of survivors. I went along initially with no greater purpose than to produce a feature for the *Listener*, where I was working. I wrote about the group, and about Lilla Wald's Hungarian mother Helen Erdos, who had survived Auschwitz and Ravensbrück. Lilla's daughter Rachel was twenty. Three generations of women talked with pain that was still fresh about the legacy of what Helen had been through.

The role of journalist can be useful for maintaining a safe distance, but when the article was published I acknowledged my background in a brief nervous disclaimer: "This story is, in part, about how the kind of massive trauma Holocaust survivors experience transmits itself to future generations. ... I was dismayed to discover that, at some deep level, I was worried that if I put it into print, if something like the Holocaust ever happened again I wouldn't be able to hide myself and my children. That seemed like a good enough reason to do it." There was metaphorical head-patting from some of my male colleagues. "Good you got that out of your system," one said.

I next wrote about my father in an essay for a book called *Mixed Blessings*, edited by a friend from the group, Deborah Knowles; it was this essay that the trauma professor from Maryland would find online.

"I can't do it," I wailed to Debbie when she rang to check on the progress of my chapter.

"Well, just tell me what you remember," she said gently. We talked for a long time. I had the chapter to her the next day.

When *Mixed Blessings* arrived at the *Listener* office in 2003 I'd been a writer there for nearly twenty years. I hadn't mentioned the book other than to ask the editor, Finlay Macdonald, for his permission to contribute to it, which he gave without hesitation.

When it came across the desk of the art and books editor, Steve Braunias, he immediately said he'd like to extract my chapter for the magazine. The support of these two colleagues, together with the kindness of strangers who wrote and shared their stories with me after the piece ran, countered the panic I had felt about exposing so much that was personal.

"I knew never to talk to you about your father," a friend said.

"Why?" I wondered, astonished.

"Because it upset you."

I'd always fought to keep in my voice steady on the rare occasions I'd talked about my father. I was sure I'd done a good job. The stories you tell yourself to get by.

There's an element of this engagement with being Jewish that can be loosely classified as "shouting at the newspaper". New Zealand, as my children are sick of hearing when we walk along a beach, is paradise. It's a lucky country with a unique indigenous culture and a vibrant diversity that was not so evident when I arrived in the more homogenised 1960s. It's also a world away from the events that nearly extinguished my father's family. I have sometimes felt stuck in a sunny suffocating South Pacific present tense. Don't look back, or forward much either. "Do we really need another movie about the Holocaust?" is a popular way to begin a film review. I shout at the paper a lot.

When Monika went on to do a communications degree, one paper required an essay about experiences of racism. She wanted to write about anti-Semitism. She was told she could write only about something she'd experienced. She said she had experienced it. No, she was told, she hadn't. There wasn't any in New Zealand.

She fought her ground, texting me for backup. Some examples are obvious. There is the desecration of Jewish cemeteries; the anti-Jewish tropes in media cartoons and letters to the editor. There's the "pity Hitler didn't finish the job" school of online commentary.

When I first came to New Zealand I heard more casual anti-Semitism than I had in Canada. "Oh, so-and-so's a bit of a Jew" might be the response when someone didn't pay for their round of drinks. My daughter was told she couldn't be Jewish because she ate bacon and didn't go to synagogue, although she had, it was kindly pointed out, the nose.

It's impossible to count the number of times I've been told that Jews run Hollywood and that a "Jewish lobby" exerts undue influence. I've had a hairdresser inform me that Jews in New York were told to stay away from work on 9/11. At a Christmas gathering a few years ago, a member of Chris's family asked me if I'd come across an amazing document he'd just discovered on the internet. *The Protocols of the Elders of Zion* are the supposed minutes of a meeting of Jewish leaders with plans for world domination through manipulating the economy, controlling the media, et cetera. I pointed out it was a notorious hoax. He didn't look convinced.

I used to think the quiet that fell when someone asked about my family background, or the subject of fathers came up, was because people didn't know what to say. I now think that some of those people just didn't want to talk about Jews. The British writer and broadcaster Laurence Rees wrote in *BBC History Magazine* about the "myth of silence". Many survivors did talk about their wartime experiences, he wrote, "though in some cases, while the survivors wanted to talk, their acquaintances and workmates were not that keen on listening."

Even in Israel the reception of survivors was deeply ambivalent.

"The desperately unfair taunt that Holocaust survivors went to their deaths like 'sheep to the slaughter' was not uncommon—a number of survivors in Israel have told me personally that they heard such insults on their arrival after the war," Rees wrote.

We visited Israel in 2016 to meet newly discovered family members on Chris's mother's side. "Where have you been?" Chris's cousin Motti said. In Jerusalem we went to Israel's great Holocaust memorial museum, Yad Vashem. Our guide talked about how the tensions between the country's heroic self-image and the perceived passivity of Holocaust victims informed the way the museum had evolved. The old museum, opened in 1957, had focused on the heroic: resistance and uprisings. Those were the stories that fitted with the ethos of a young assertive country. Canadian Israeli architect Moshe Safdie's new museum, dedicated in 2005, highlights the stories of victims and survivors. Two and a half thousand personal items, from letters to artwork, ensure the lost have names.

The 1961 Eichmann trial in Jerusalem had proved pivotal, forcing the world to pay attention to the demented mechanics of the Third Reich's genocidal mission. "There exist many things considerably worse than death, and the S.S. saw to it that none of them was ever very far from the mind and imagination of their victims," Hannah Arendt wrote in *The New Yorker* in 1963 of Eichmann's trial. In such a situation no victim is passive: they are actively occupied in staying alive minute to minute when taking action, or not taking action, can mean instant death.

Journalism offered me rare chances to hear raw testimony first-hand. I spoke to the Nobel prize-winning chemist Roald Hoffmann for a profile in 2013. He was born in Złoczów, Poland, and survived the war hidden with his mother in an attic by a Ukrainian teacher. "I've just been looking at the behaviour of German physicists before World War II as one-quarter of their colleagues were fired from university jobs and they did nothing," he said. When we got on to his life in hiding as a young child, he spoke for a while and then said, "Let's talk of other things."

In 2015, at her home in London, Hungarian Susan Pollack talked to me about surviving Auschwitz as a thirteen-year-old. She had just testified at the trial of Oskar Gröning, the so-called "Bookkeeper of Auschwitz". Gröning claimed to accept "moral guilt" but there's always slippage when former Nazis talk about remorse. In a 2005 BBC interview he had described a scene at the camp. "A child who was lying there was simply pulled by the legs and chucked into a truck to be driven away. And when it screamed like a sick chicken, they then bashed it against the edge of the truck so it would shut up." A witness at the trial offered Gröning forgiveness. Susan Pollack did not. "I couldn't do it. I could not embrace him. I don't forgive the perpetrators. They knew what they were doing."

Publishing on the Holocaust yields interesting mail. There was the polite enquiry, when I wrote about the Treblinka death camp, seeking the sources "for [the writer's] assertion that 'Guards were allowed to grab babies and smash their heads on the boxcars'." I was busy composing a reply, citing the numerous sources, not least the testimony of perpetrators like Oskar Gröning, when Chris said, "Don't engage with them. It's not worth it." He's had his share. "I have to wonder if you are a Jew of the Zionist persuasion," a reader wrote in response to a story Chris published in *The New Zealand Herald* about Holocaust memorials. It was suggested he should "investigate who runs the world today. The same ones who ran it then."

Another correspondent began with some bland academic questions before inquiring, "When have the Jews ever told the truth about anything?" America's dropping of the atom bomb on two Japanese cities was, he claimed, "a Jewish-initiated holocaust".

Yet another cited the work of discredited Holocaust deniers as evidence there were no gas chambers. "You are either very out-of-date or under some foreign control." The lengths denialists go to in their efforts to distort the truth become, paradoxically, a testament to the enduring power of the crime they are so desperate to refute.

The historian Ann Beaglehole has pointed out that the New Zealand government limited the numbers of Jewish refugees admitted during the rise of Hitler. "Non-Jewish applicants are regarded as a more suitable type of immigrant," Edwin Dudley Good, comptroller of customs, noted. Walter Nash, minister of customs in the country's first Labour administration, which took office in 1936, argued: "There is a major difficulty of absorbing these people in our cultural life without raising a feeling of antipathy to them." Also "anti-Semitism, never far from the surface, [is] very apt to emerge in the case of the talented race whose members can often beat us at our own game, especially the game of money making."

Discounting of prejudice doesn't make it go away. "I really wonder about anti-Semitism," mused a *New Zealand Herald* columnist in 2004. "Anti-Semitism died the day the victors of World War II opened the Nazi death camps." He had possibly never read about the Polish survivors who, when they tried to go home in 1946, were subjected to hostility, violence, and in the case of the town of Kielce mass murder: forty-two men women and children were mostly beaten and stoned to death.

Anti-Semitism is having a resurgence in Europe, as *The Atlantic* magazine pointed out in a 2015 story entitled "Is It Time for the Jews to Leave Europe?" In France in 2014 fifty-one percent of all racist attacks were against Jews. Two days after the Charlie Hebdo massacre in January 2015, a kosher grocery store in Paris was attacked and four hostages killed because they were Jewish. In the UK, the British Labour Party under Jeremy Corbyn has been forced to address anti-Semitism within its ranks.

The column in the *Herald* was about desecration at Wellington's Makara Cemetery, where Jewish headstones had been pushed over and a prayer pavilion set on fire. A swastika had been etched on the pavilion's wall and another gouged into the grass. Strangely, the columnist saw himself as the real victim: "I am almost afraid now to argue for the freedom of a Holocaust sceptic to visit here or even criticise Israel as strongly as it deserves," he wrote, concluding: "Israel and its apologists will continue to need the anachronism of anti-Semitism to silence critics and manipulate public opinion."

The "sceptic" referred to was David Irving, a notorious Holocaust denier who had for some reason been invited to address the National Press Club in Wellington. It was an odd description of someone who once said, "More women died on the back seat of Edward Kennedy's car at Chappaquiddick than in the gas chambers at Auschwitz."

Then there was the curious case of the Canterbury University MA student Joel Hayward. Irving had been one of Hayward's sources for his 1993 MA thesis, which concluded that "the weight of evidence supports the view that the Nazis did not systematically exterminate Jews in gas chambers" and that a "careful and impartial investigation of the available evidence pertaining to Nazi gas chambers reveals that these apparently fall into the category of atrocity propaganda."

The thesis was awarded an A+. The New Zealand Jewish Council asked Richard Evans, a historian of modern Germany at Cambridge University, to give his opinion on its academic merits. "What I found was very shocking," Evans responded. "The Holocaust denial literature Dr Hayward was considering was well known to specialists and others as anti-Semitic, racist and frequently neo-fascist propaganda masquerading as scholarship."

The A+ still stands, although the thesis now has an addendum by Hayward addressing its "flaws". There was good work on the debacle by a few local journalists, but a disappointing number chose to see the affair as an attack on academic freedom, rather than a laughable failure of academic standards. A journalist in *The Dominion Post* warned, in a pro-Hayward piece, of a possible backlash against the Jewish community.

In 2015 a University of Auckland professor, Scott Poynting, sent a letter to the *Waikato Times* in which he compared the employment of Palestinians by an Israeli company, SodaStream, to a German company employing Jews during the Second World War. "Thank you for explaining in your article how SodaStream generously provided work for Palestinians," Poynting wrote. "I understand that IG Farben provided work for large numbers of Jews. Not that I have anything against Germans, mind you." IG Farben made the gas used by the Nazis to exterminate Jews. The university took no action.

HAVING CHILDREN AND GRANDCHILDREN changes your relationship to the living and the dead. I worry about the effect on them of my Holocaust preoccupations. I worry about their DNA. There's evidence that trauma can be transmitted to future generations and alter their stress hormones. As science magazine *Discover* put it in a headline, "Grandma's experiences leave a mark on your genes." Once, interviewing geneticist and author Richard Dawkins, I took the opportunity to quiz him about this. "Oh," he said dismissively, "maybe for a generation or two but it's not a permanent change."

I have quizzed my children about any collateral damage. For my son, the family history is just one strand of his identity. "I don't remember ever not knowing about it. I've certainly told people the story. I'd say it means just as much as any other part of my heritage." For my daughter, it's a strong part of who she is. In every generation one child may take the role of what psychologist Dina Wardi calls the family's "memorial candle".

My stepson, who has grown up with my family's story and recently discovered more about his own Jewish roots, teases her about her enthusiastic embrace of her Jewishness. He thinks of Jewishness as a religion not an ethnicity, but recently cooked Chris and me our first ever Passover Seder dinner.

Around the time I heard my father had died, my English course at university included Bernard Malamud's *The Assistant*, about a Jewish immigrant shopkeeper in post-war Brooklyn, and *The Fixer*, about anti-Semitism in Tsarist Russia. The books stirred old memories, and once after a class I tried to talk to the lecturer, mentioning my family history. He looked at me as though I were mad. Perhaps I was. There were no trigger warnings in those days. Every once in a while, I would be ambushed by suppressed grief. My hand would shoot up: "My father's family were murdered by the Nazis." It never went well. I learned to shut up.

CHAPTER 10

Visitors from New York

Mr Wichtel has been very independent and is hurt and confused by the rejection of both his wife and his brother.

Miss Crawford, Brockville, May 8, 1968

IN THE WINTER OF 1987 Sy's widow Auntie Mollie and my cousin Linda fly back into our lives. Chris and I are now living in Devonport with my son Ben, who is ten. Chris's Ben, aged six, is with us every second weekend and during holidays. We are what our therapist likes to call a "reconstituted family undergoing a process of recalibration". We are a family with three different surnames and two children called Ben. Mum and Stew, back from Japan, are living close by. After Mollie tracks down Mum, she and Linda are on the next plane. The door to our other life across the world is about to open. Realities prepare to collide. I assume the brace position.

EARLIER THAT YEAR CHRIS AND I had taken the boys on a trip to Vancouver. It was the first time I'd been back since we left in 1964. We had visited Stanley Park, scene of our happiest family outings, where the sight of a squirrel had triggered a wave of nostalgia. A moment later the grass was seething with them, like something from a Hitchcock movie. The return to Vancouver felt like that: too many squirrels, too many ghosts.

I ran up and down Pender Street like a lunatic searching for English Textiles, even though I knew the old tenements had been torn down not long before. We met Auntie Rose and Uncle Harry, who were still in the same house, and had dinner at a restaurant with them and Rose's sisters Ida and Ethel.

Dread set in as we drove back to their house for coffee. Christmas decorations were everywhere. My father hadn't let us have lights on the outside of our place, declaring them vulgar, although in the last year or two he had relented and put up a single string.

"Of course he didn't have Christmas lights," Rose said. "He was Jewish."

I didn't say there was never any mention of Hanukkah, or that, when I insist on Christmas lights on our house every year, it's as a kind of tribute to my father.

He had no objection to decorations inside. We always had the most impressive Christmas tree in the street strategically placed in the front window of the living room. The oil inside the lights on the tree bubbled when the lights heated up, intensifying the piney smell. There was always the Sputnik ornament, because we children were going to fly to the moon.

On that trip to Vancouver, I found I remembered Rose and Harry's little house by heart. There was the spare room with the piano, where we used to play increasingly elaborate versions of "Heart and Soul", and the small garden where we sat on hot afternoons having iced tea and watermelon. There was the magic cupboard full of gifts so no visitor ever left empty-handed. We ate the chocolate cake, thawed from the freezer, that we had never really liked because it wasn't iced. And then there was the kitsch collection of salt and pepper shakers, most of which would now be considered culturally inappropriate. There was the chair where my father would sit, arguing about politics, the Studebaker parked outside. I excused myself, went to the bathroom and took a Valium.

Rose changed the subject every time I tried to talk about my father. Harry, who used to make us laugh by singing "Donald Where's Your Troosers?", who wanted to teach us Hebrew, took me aside. "Your father was very sick," he said. "We tried to help him but he wouldn't let us. Everyone tried to help." He didn't judge my mother for leaving. He knew how hard she'd tried.

Did he know whether my father was ever really meant to follow us to New Zealand? "I don't know what happened to him after he moved east," he said. I could see he was worried I might think they should have done more, might blame them for what had happened. I hugged him and told him I knew he was a good friend to my father. I knew he had done his best.

As we headed for the airport before dawn I made the taxi driver go to 3389 West 43rd Street, Kerrisdale, the house where we had been happy. I jumped out and tried to get some photos in the pitch dark. When the photos were developed they were blank.

MUM HAS PICKED UP MOLLIE AND LINDA from the Regent Hotel. Mollie likes to go in style, although she's no longer as well off as she once was. She's in her seventies, a few years older than Mum, and looks good—maybe she's had a little work done. She's smaller than I remember and no longer scary. Linda is warm, pretty and has a way with children, talking to them as equals. Our boys fall instantly in love with her.

Mollie is quick to say that they tried to help my father. Like Harry she seems worried we might blame them. I know how much Sy did, I tell her.

I'm worried how this invasion of the past into the present will go.

Stew is drinking a lot and things can get out of hand. As it turns out, Mollie still likes a drink, Stew is funny and charming, and Linda and I talk a little about our dead fathers. Mollie tells my mother she did the right thing by leaving. She says she herself should have left Sy much earlier than she did.

After Mollie and Linda go back to New York, we keep in touch by letter. I beg Mollie to tell me anything she knows about the Wichtel family. She lists the family traits she saw in my father and Sy: "impetuous, impulsive, stubborn and extremely sensitive."

"You and Jerry are the tallest Wichtels," she writes. "He's six feet two and I understand you had a tall grandfather." I guess that would be Dad's father. Some of his mother's family, the Joniszes, were very small. By the age of twelve I was taller than my father.

There was a lot of collateral damage in their family as well as ours. Jerry had some tough years: estrangement from Sy, who was alcoholic and abusive, then drug and drinking problems of his own. "Difficult to watch? Yes," Mollie writes, "but he picked himself up— the Wichtel genes are strong—and applied himself to the business of living."

Like Mum, Mollie had to go out to work when times got tough. She got a job in a department store. Sy outlived my father by only seven years. One day he fell down in the street. He had a brain tumour. There was not much that could be done. Mollie visited him in hospital, as did a former girlfriend and his current girlfriend—all his women except Lillian, his first wife. "I no longer walk in Abraham's world," she said when told he was sick.

Sy had his family with him in 1977 as he was dying. Linda tells me he said to Mollie, "Thank you for the children." Mollie said, "Thank you for the best years of my life."

My mother would always say, "When you children were small, those were the happiest years of my life."

Wedding portrait of Sy Wichtel and his second wife Mollie.

I ASK MOLLIE IF SHE KNOWS ANYTHING about Dad, what happened to his papers, where he ended up. She doesn't. She and Sy were falling apart at the time. She does provide one unbearable detail. One day after we left for New Zealand my father turned up unannounced at their home in New Jersey. He ran through the house calling out our names.

I'm grateful Mollie and Linda got on a plane to New Zealand. I'm grateful, too, that I got to see Rose and Harry one last time in

Vancouver. I've been back there three times now. I know what's what. Yet each time I'm gripped with the same crazy thinking, the sort Joan Didion scrupulously recorded in her memoir *The Year of Magical Thinking* about her brain's inability to absorb the sudden death of her husband. "We do not expect to be literally crazy, cool customers who believe their husband is about to return and need his shoes," she wrote. I never expect to find myself roaming Pender Street, sure that if I just look hard enough what's gone will still be there somewhere, hiding in a crack in time. But it's always the same. There I am, Dad, half-believing I will come across you outside English Textiles, just standing there smoking a cigarette and watching the world go by.

CHAPTER 11

"Er iz a krank mentsch"

Patient served with the "Underground" in Warsaw, Poland from 1939
until 1945. ... He stated that he was always very close to his family, but
recalls many hardships and heartbreaking experiences during the War years.
Clinical record, Brockville Psychiatric Hospital, May 26, 1967

KEEN TO KEEP UP CONTACT with our newly rediscovered family, Chris
and I see Mollie and Linda again in New York in 1990, at the tail end
of a writing trip for the *Listener.* This is in the days when a journalist
and photographer are put up in a hotel in London's Marble Arch to
interview stars of British television shows: big hair, bigger shoulder
pads, and an expense account.

We meet Linda after work and go to her local bar, the sort of place
where everybody knows your name, and then to her studio apartment.
Over vodka we make another assault on that inexhaustible topic, our
fathers. We're beginning to talk more freely but the excavation of this
particular archaeological site is slow and careful, layer by fragile layer.

Uncle Sy adored his daughter. She was exempt from his violent
rages. "He'd have a fight with my brother, throw him out of the house.
Have a fight with my mother, she'd go running to a hotel. He'd come
into my room and say, 'My life is in the palm of your hand.'" Linda
thinks she reminded him of the mother he loved so much and couldn't

119

save. It's a common experience: children born after the Shoah standing in for the dead.

It's on this trip that we reconnect with Jerry. The tall handsome cousin who showed me his bar mitzvah gifts has become a successful Wall Street trader. We meet at Harry's, a bar in the financial district. He tells us of his days of single malt whisky and closing bars. Before that he did drugs. Now he doesn't drink.

Chris and I order a couple of stiff ones. Jerry says, "I have to tell you, I don't do family." We will find out he has his reasons, and that sometimes he is willing to make an exception. Now he says, "A lot of people went through hell. It doesn't mean you have to be an asshole." I value his honesty, startling at first. After so rocky a road it seems Jerry is lucky to have survived.

He takes us on to the floor of the stock exchange and shows us around, and then we meet up with Mollie, Linda, and Jerry's partner Jill, a social worker who instantly offers friendship and good advice about staring down the guilt: "You were just a child. You didn't get a vote." We go to dinner at Windows on the World, the famous restaurant in the north tower of the World Trade Centre. It's a long way up. It's the middle of summer and there are problems with the air conditioning. The stern rule about men wearing a jacket is relaxed. When the air finally cools, a waiter issues an oblique command: "The gentlemen are putting on their jackets now."

Auntie Mollie orders poularde. God knows what we order. Being here with the Wichtel family, who have become like fictional characters in a story that could surely never have happened, combines with the dizzy view to cause an existential vertigo. Ten years later we will watch like the rest of the world as the towers and the people in them are wiped out by a different set of lunatics from the ones our family encountered. A chance change of schedule will mean Jerry is not in the building.

IN JUNE 2006 CHRIS AND I ARE BACK IN NEW YORK again for a few days. On this trip we bring our daughter Monika, who is now fourteen and has never met any of her New York family. We visit the ruined site of the twin towers and read the heartbreaking notes still on the fences. Our travel itineraries will become increasingly prone to include mass graves. Jerry and Jill come over from their place in New Jersey and take us to the Museum of Modern Art for lunch. Just as Uncle Sy once made me try caviar, his son makes Monika try foie gras. After lunch we prowl the gallery, half an eye on the art but mostly we talk about our families. Since we were here last Auntie Mollie has died. Linda has adopted a baby girl and named her Mollie. When we meet Mollie she is a beautiful, funny, clever eleven-year-old. Linda and Mollie now live in an apartment in a nice part of town. It's also home to a cat and a bouncy tangerine-coloured dog called Peanut.

It's on the last day of the visit that Linda tells me about Joe. "You know, we have another cousin," she says. Joe Lubell turns out to be my father's first cousin, the younger son of his Aunt Sabina. Born in Brooklyn, New York in 1930, Joe was about seventeen when the family's survivors began to arrive in America from Europe. He met my father. Why didn't I know about Joe before? Why didn't he know about us? "There is only looking," Daniel Mendelsohn writes in *The Lost*, "and finally seeing what was always there."

I might have put two and two together earlier if I hadn't come from a family with so many painful mysteries that the only response to them was a sort of self-protective paralysis. I knew my father had a cousin called Estelle. She was the pretty young woman who stayed with us when I was four years old, with her toddler Babette who spoke with a Brooklyn accent. I never heard my father refer to Estelle again. I never thought to ask where she had materialised from and disappeared to.

Sabina Lubell, sister of Rozalia and mother of Joe, with her daughter Estelle.

Sabina, the sister of my grandmother Rozalia, had come to America via France with her husband, Albert Lubell, in the 1920s. She had died in Far Rockaway, Queens, in February 1982. She had outlived her two nephews Ben and Sy. Why hadn't I known about her either?

I learn that Sabina had a lot of tragedy in her life. Her first son Solomon, one of Joe's two brothers, had died at the age of five, struck by a car while chasing a ball. Her daughter Estelle, once a beauty queen, Miss Brooklyn, had married a wealthy Canadian, Hy Singer of the sewing machine family, but the marriage had collapsed. Perhaps Estelle had just separated from her husband when she visited us in Vancouver. In 1991 she had died in a house fire.

When I learn about Joe, he is living in Allentown, Pennsylvania. Linda is the only one of the Wichtel family in touch with him. I rush back to the hotel. Forget packing: I have Joe's phone number.

Hearing his voice is like being dragged backwards through a tunnel in time. "Your father and I were first cousins," he says. "We carry the same DNA."

He tells me his mother Sabina and his cousin Sy were close for a long time. Sy would visit Sabina on weekends, bring her presents. They would talk together in Yiddish. They were in cahoots. Joe knew him as Uncle Eddy, and later as Abe. "When I was a child he sat with me on the living-room floor of our modest apartment in Brooklyn playing chess," he says. "When he left he gave me five dollars, which was a fortune in those Great Depression days. You could see the Brooklyn Dodgers at Ebbets Field for fifty cents. An ice-cream cone or a hot dog was five cents."

Joe, with his Brooklyn accent, doesn't sound like my father but he talks in the heightened way my father did, with a little extra humour, a little extra drama. Bluntly, with a trace of Yiddish. "You know Yiddish was my first language," he says. He was held back when he first went to school because he couldn't speak English. "My mother spoke Yiddish to me. It drove me crazy."

Joe worked for Sy at his luggage factory for a while. His older brother, Jack, worked there for longer and got a good wage on the proviso fifteen dollars a week went to his mother.

Sy met and married his first wife, Lillian, in America. After Sy divorced her and married Mollie, relations with Joe's side of the family seem to have become strained. Sy and Mollie went to Joe's wedding—there's a photo of them with the handsome young couple, smiling—but sometime after that the families drifted apart. Sy was becoming a wealthy man and moving in different circles. Linda tells me that before Sy died she took him for a final visit to Sabina at Far Rockaway. "Such a young man," Sabina said.

Joe says that when my father arrived in New York he visited Sabina. She was his only remaining aunt. Contact seems to have continued for

Wedding portrait of Sy Wichtel and his first wife Lillian.

a while: Joe has photos that Dad may have sent to Sabina, or perhaps to Sy who passed them on. But it seems he didn't stay in touch. Why not? Such a small family left but the centre could not hold.

I HAVE SO MANY QUESTIONS FOR JOE, so little time. In his seventies when we first make contact, he is a force of nature, a difficult man to interrupt. He begins immediately to write to me about our family and send photographs. There is one of my great-grandmother Brandla Jonisz, another of my great-grandfather Chaim Jakob Jonisz, known as Yankel, who died before the war. There is a picture of Estelle at twenty-one, stylish in a fur coat from her father's business.

I beg Joe for a photograph of his mother, my Great-aunt Sabina. Joe and his wife Barbara tell me a little of her story. Sabina had been the last unmarried daughter in the family, unable to land a husband, schlepping sacks of potatoes for her father's business. Albert, dragooned into the Russian counter-revolutionary army, had deserted. In Warsaw he met and proposed to Sabina. The couple married in Germany, lived in France, and emigrated to the US in the 1920s.

Joe sends a photo of Sabina from her later years. An orthodox Jewish lady, she wears a wig and a pink satin blouse, and stares staunchly at the camera. I scan her face, searching for resemblances. I can see a likeness to my father's mother. I can see my father and a little of myself. She has a mole on the bridge of her nose like me and my father. I was thirty-two when she died. I could have met her if only I'd known. If I wish to drive myself crazy that's one of the things I think about. Chasing the past is a recurring bad dream, the kind where you always get there just too late.

At least I haven't been too late to find Joe. "My mother would have mothered you because you are a Wichtel," he writes, "made you chicken soup with noodles, kneidlach matzo balls, served you some form of chicken.

Albert and Sabina Lubell, parents of Solomon, Estelle, Jack and Joseph (Joe), New York.

"My father didn't speak very much, but if he took a liking to you you would get a fur coat, or maybe a muff, or maybe a fur neck piece." I suddenly remember that my mother had a lambswool coat, the mink that Mollie had sent, and a fox fur stole I still have. They probably came from Albert Lubell's business.

"My mother could be an aggressive strong-minded woman," Joe writes. "She was Yiddish in outlook and a religious Jew. It was best not to be anti-religious when she was around. She had a guilt complex about leaving Poland and having almost her entire family killed. I am very sorry you never met them. They were honest hardworking immigrants. We cannot undo what is passed."

But to undo what has passed is exactly what I want. Finding Joe seems a miracle, so why not more miracles?

The next year, 2007, I meet Joe in person at the bat mitzvah of Linda's daughter Mollie. The ceremony takes place in December. My son comes along and also my stepson, who is living in New York. My sister Ros and her son Karl complete the New Zealand contingent. From Canada, there is my brother Jeff, his wife Maureen, and their daughters Jocelyn and Nicola.

The sight of our boys wearing yarmulkes for the ceremony as my father had for Jerry's makes me cry. I am undone again when they front up to do the duty of the strong and nerveless during the circle dance known as the hora, lifting Mollie and Linda high on chairs. There is to be a cousins' reunion next day at the home of Joe's brother Jack, but a blizzard blows in. A longer meeting will have to wait. But Linda has achieved what no one has for nearly fifty years: a formal event uniting the remnants of our two families.

JOE KEEPS UP A CONSTANT FLOW OF INFORMATION. I learn the family lived in Praga, a suburb of Warsaw on the east side of the river Vistula. "You can imagine if there was no World War II and no slaughter of our family how large and dispersed our family would be. I consider the New Zealand branch very important in preserving the remnants of the Jonisz family," Joe writes.

Names that exist on no official list arrive. I learn that my grandmother Rozalia was one of ten children of Brandla and Yankel Jonisz. She married Jacob Joseph Wichtel, started her family at the age of sixteen, had seven children and was widowed in 1928.

Her sister Dora was married to Bernard Gastman, who had a shoe factory. They had five children. Her brother Salomon, a clerk at City Hall in Warsaw, married Bernard's sister Dina. They had two children: Dora, one of our family's three survivors of the Holocaust, and her younger sister.

Herszel was a vegetable dealer like his father Yankel. It's not known how many children he had with his wife Maria. As for the tenth child, there are mentions of a Maria, married to a military man, and

Yankel Jonisz and Brandla Jonisz, Warsaw, Poland, dates unknown.

a Joseph, who was a cantor, but we can't be sure. Berl (Bernard), wife unknown, had two children, ran a flour business and possibly had a farm. Faiga's husband ran a hardware business and had the surname Pel. They had one child. Nothing is known of Szymon except that, like my father, he was in textiles. Sabina ended up in Brooklyn. Pawel (Paul) survived the war in Poland.

These great-aunts and -uncles had a total of twenty-six children. Some of those children had children of their own, whose names we will never know. All in Poland would die in the war except for my father, his cousin Dora and his uncle Paul. Four generations, almost entirely erased.

After the Germans invaded Poland in 1939 the family in America had had some contact with their relatives in Warsaw. "We received a distress letter in Brooklyn," Joe tells me. "It was in Yiddish. They wanted help to get out of Poland. The whole thing was impossible, at the time, to move such a huge family."

Sabina and Albert went to the Hebrew Immigrant Aid Society and asked for help. "The society tried, but then the Germans ordered that all Jews had to go to a ghetto and they cut off all communication at that point to the outside world." Sabina could never talk about her lost family. "My mother crying before the large photos of her mother and father which hung in her bedroom I will never forget. She knew they were doomed."

There is one last letter from the ghetto that still exists. Joe would have been eleven when his mother received it in 1941.

From the end of 1940 Warsaw's Jews have been forced to live behind a wall up to ten feet high and topped with barbed wire and broken glass. They have been made to pay for the wall. The average daily food ration per person is 184 calories.

By 1941 the Einsatzgruppen, special units following the German army east, are systematically slaughtering Jews. They have a model in the pogroms of Eastern Europe. These pogroms also carry on, often with minimal help from the Nazis. In July 1941 up to 1,600 Jews—men, women, children and babies—are murdered by their neighbours in the Polish town of Jedwabne. After being subjected to taunts, humiliations, beatings and rape, most are locked in a barn and burned alive.

The sender of the last letter is my Great-aunt Faiga Pel. My father had told me there were twins in his family. When I look at the dates Joe has sent I see that his mother, Sabina, was born in 1898. So was Faiga. Sabina and Faiga were twins. The address is Pawia 61/56: Flat 61, 56 Peacock Street. It has come via the Lisbon office of HICEM, a Jewish aid organisation set up in 1927 to help European Jews emigrate.

It is signed by an official of the ghetto's Judenrat, one of the Jewish councils set up by the Nazis. Such councils worked to help their fellow Jews but were forced by the Nazis to take part in organising their destruction. The system created what Primo Levi called the "gray zone", a territory of ambiguity, of morality tipped upside down.

Some of their leaders, like Łódź Ghetto's infamous chairman Chaim Rumkowski, made obscene calculations—give up some for deportation in the hope of saving others who could work. In September 1942 Rumkowski gave one of the most terrible speeches in the history of human communication. Ordered to organise the handover of the old and the children to the Nazis, he said: "Brothers and sisters, give them to me. Give me your children … Children above ten are saved. Let that at least be some consolation in your great pain." When faced with a similar order in July that year, the head of the Warsaw Ghetto's Judenrat, Adam Czerniaków, had committed suicide in despair.

Sara Plagier, sixteen, gives an account of the deportation. "I saw two wagons full of little children drive past the open gate. Many of the children were dressed in their holiday best, the little girls with coloured ribbons in their hair. In spite of the soldiers in their midst, the children were shrieking at the top of their lungs. They were calling out for their mothers."

The message from Faiga Pel to her twin sister Sabina is couched in the elaborately analgesic language allowed to those who have lost all human rights and whose words will be censored by their oppressors. "We ask politely to transmit from your sister thanks for the package which she received. She asked for further packages and mother asks for packages. The packages should be sent to Brandla Jonisz. Best greetings—sends her love and thank you very much, and asking for an answer soon by airmail." "We ask politely"; "soon by airmail": what desperation bleeds through those formal greetings.

The only way to know something of what my family endured is through written accounts of the ghetto. Abraham Lewin, a school teacher, recorded the daily horrors in his diary, later published as a book, *A Cup of Tears*: "They emptied Dr Korczak's orphanage with the Doctor at the head. Two hundred orphans… Many victims on Miła Street… In the evening a pogrom in the streets. A great many killed at various locations—Smocza, Pawia, Miła, Zamenhof and others."

Faiga lived on Pawia Street, my father on Miła. Film from the time shows long lines of men loading emaciated naked bodies on wheelbarrows to take to mass graves. Adam Czerniaków described the starvation and sickness. "At 63 Pawia Street 450 people have died." Faiga and many more of my family were at number 56.

The German word for relief packages sent to the ghetto was "Liebesgabenpakete"—"Love gifts". We will never know if Brandla received the next love gifts from her family in New York. But we do know something of what was happening in the ghetto at the time Faiga sent her letter. "The Germans came, rounding up people every day," survivor Zosia Goldberg wrote in her memoir *Running Through Fire*. "One day they said, 'Everyone who is a redhead will go.' Then the next day, 'Everyone who is freckled.' Another day, those with kinky hair; another, those with the Jewish nose; another, those who look like Gentiles; another, those who look beautiful. Then, those who are ugly, those with bow legs. Too old. All pregnant women. All women with little children. All men..."

Faiga's letter is now in the United States Holocaust Memorial Museum, with other Jonisz family material that Joe carefully kept over the years. He emailed me a copy. On the front is an official stamp bearing the Nazi emblem of a black eagle above an oak wreath, with a swastika at its centre. It is dated June 26, 1941. Two months later, on August 29, Brandla Jonisz had died of starvation, having given most of her rations to the younger ones. Joe tells me his family learned of Brandla's fate from my father when he arrived in New York in 1947. I think of what he told me about his time in the ghetto: "You wake up and the person next to you is dead."

JOE TELLS ME WHAT I MOST WANT TO KNOW—the story of my father. "Ben Wichtel was a young, very athletic man," he writes. "They were en

Jewish partisans in a forest in the Lublin area, where Ben Wichtel was liberated at the end of the war. He was with partisans and others who had escaped from ghettos and the nearby Majdanek concentration camp.

route to Treblinka, which was not a concentration camp but a killing centre about two hours north of Warsaw. There the Nazis established gas chambers to kill the Jews. Ben Wichtel jumped off the train."

The trains had little windows with barbed wire but my father managed to get out. "He must have been very thin to do that," Joe says.

He lived in the forest until the end of the war. I will learn from his post-liberation registration card, and from a list made when he was liberated, that he was with found with partisans and others who had escaped from ghettos and from the Majdanek concentration camp near Lublin.

Did he fight? I ask Joe. "Of course he fought! He wouldn't have survived if he didn't fight."

Joe tells me that after the war Sy searched and searched for family members, but after he found Ben the reunion in New York didn't go well. "Your father came to my house with a guitar. Which was the wrong thing to do, by the way," Joe says. He looked bohemian, not what was expected. He looked merry. "I can't explain it. He looked fine. He didn't look like he had a problem in the world.

"Everybody pleaded with him to stay in the New York area and everything would be fine, they would take care of him. Because he wasn't all put together, you know. If you get out of the ghetto and all this crazy running around, you don't expect to be perfectly stable. Jumping off the train, living like an animal for three years with a little terrorist group who ran around and tried to knock off Germans or steal things to survive…"

I had somehow imagined my father had just hidden in a box under the ground until liberation, but of course that could never have been true. He was young, strong, smart, and he had to eat, he had to live, had to fight. As my daughter Monika will put it, "That's some *Inglourious Basterds* shit."

We know only fragments of what my father saw and did. In Laurence Rees' book *The Holocaust*, survivor Dario Gabbai talks about an SS guard, Otto Moll, who was particularly sadistic, even by the standards of Auschwitz. He liked to kill naked girls by shooting them "on their breasts", the sort of scene my father had described.

What did my father have to do to survive? I might have been frightened of his rages but I had known him as a gentle man, opposed to violence. In my narrative he was a passive victim, but on this sort of voyage everything you think you know can turn out to be wrong.

To Joe, he was maddeningly stubborn. "Why in the hell didn't he stay in New York? It didn't make sense fifty years ago. It doesn't make sense today."

Everyone tried to persuade him to stay. Sy was making a lot of money. He had had government contracts during the war and his luggage business was going well. "He made your father a wonderful offer," Joe says. "He was a very kind man and a very generous man. He was outstanding in intelligence and elegance.

"My mother pleaded with him in Yiddish. He was going so far away. It wasn't around the corner. He would pay attention to no one. Your father was very handsome, musically talented and well spoken, all assets which would benefit him. Our family didn't understand his move far off to Canada." He recalled having once heard that my father may have been going to join a woman he'd met in a displaced persons camp.

On the positive side, Joe says, if Ben hadn't gone to Vancouver he wouldn't have met my mother. "And you and I wouldn't be talking now."

Sy, who had supported my father so far, arranged to send him money every month.

JOE UNDERSTANDS WHAT WAR CAN DO: he served in Korea in the 1950s, working with severely wounded soldiers in hospital, an experience that affected him deeply. He has spent years of his life researching and teaching about what happened to our family and all the Jews of Nazi-occupied Europe. Nearly every time we talk he says, "God, how I hate those Nazi bastards." His anger remains white-hot for his aunts and uncles and their children, for Rachele and Brandla, and for the survivors. "Your dad went through hell and back and never recovered from the Holocaust. He ran away from Jewishness, his heritage and his family."

After my father left his aunt's house in New York, Sabina said something that made an impression on seventeen-year-old Joe: "Er iz a krank mentsh"—He is a sick man. When she heard years later that my father was dead, she believed he had killed himself.

Joe and Barbara Lubell's wedding in Brooklyn, New York, 1953. Standing, left to right: Sy and Mollie Wichtel, Lillian and Paul Jonisz; seated, Joe and Barbara.

135

The things Joe has told me suggest there was an unbridgeable gulf between the family members who, during the war, had been helpless and distraught but safe in America and those who turned up afterwards, having walked out of hell.

Dad's Uncle Paul, who had survived by hiding out on the Aryan side of Warsaw, stayed in New York. "Uncle Paul wasn't that good-looking," Joe says, "but he had a certain… When he met you he'd take your hand, hold your hand and kiss it, and bow European style. Women just loved that stuff." I remember the look in my mother's eyes when she talked about how my father had courted her, kissing her hands and clicking his heels.

My father was twenty-nine when the war started. I ask Joe if he was married. Joe says he wasn't. Later, during one of our long phone conversations, I ask him if he knows why. Possibly it was the hard times, he says. Maybe my father didn't feel he could take on a wife. "Jewish women weren't the easiest women to seduce and have sex with. That's the way it was. You couldn't have sex with them. You know men solve their problem by masturbation. … Why are you laughing? That's what they do."

My father's cousin Dora, the family's youngest and only female survivor, ended up in Mexico but remained in touch with Joe and Barbara. They tell me what they know of her story. She was nineteen when the war began. One day she managed to leave the ghetto to get medicine for her mother. While outside, she met a school friend who was a Catholic. The friend offered her the baptismal papers of her dead sister. When she told her mother, her mother told her to do whatever she could do to save herself.

She left the ghetto and was helped by the friend's family. "She passed as a Christian," Joe says. "The Nazis were looking for Jewish girls but you can't tell a Jewish girl because Jewish girls aren't circumcised like Jewish boys. A Jewish boy they would simply pull his pants down and if they saw the penis circumcised they would kill him. It's easy to forget how terrible they were. They were animalistic. The whole thing is just a horror."

Later Dora was rounded up with other girls by the Germans and sent to work in a factory.

PAUL WAS MARKED BY HIS EXPERIENCES. He became paranoid. "It isn't difficult for me to understand why Uncle Paul, walking down the street with me in New York and suddenly looking at a New York City police car, said 'Polizei!' and became very upset," Joe says. "He was having a flashback of his life in Europe when he was on the run."

Paul had seen his first wife slaughtered in the street. He had met his second wife, Lillian, in a displaced persons camp. She was a survivor of Auschwitz who had been subjected to medical experiments. "Dr Mengele—do you know who he was?—Mengele used X-rays on women's ovaries to see how much X-ray it took to make women unable to bear children."

Possibly as a result of these experiments, Lillian died young of cancer. When she was in hospital, Barbara would visit her.

She told me Paul would take Joe for a walk so he could tell him "they" knew where he was and were following him. "Even though Paul managed to escape, he was not left undamaged. That is why, when he closed his business, he and Lillian went to Mexico."

The past he had so hopefully left behind returned for Paul, just as it would for my father. "Later on he was not all put together" is how Joe put it. After Lillian died, Joe heard from a Jewish agency in Mexico to which Paul had gone for help. Joe and Barbara wired money and the agency put Paul on a plane to New York. He was again a displaced person.

Barbara found him a place in a Jewish retirement home. "That was a mistake," Joe tells me. "I didn't know he really didn't like Jews. Who could figure that out?" A rabbi came to visit and told Paul he didn't want him to play the radio or watch television on Saturday, Shabbat. "An argument ensued and Uncle Paul took a chair and whacked the rabbi. So yeah, it was quite a scene," Joe says. "I went down to the police station and talked to them and had to pay $200 to get him out of jail."

Joe and Barbara found Paul a place in a home run by Italian Catholics. "He loved it there because there were very few men, mostly women, and the women would try and take care of him." Joe was Paul's guardian. "We took care of him until the day he died. Well, I loved him."

JOE SAYS THERE'S NO POINT trying to figure out why my father didn't stay with what little family he had left. "You, as a daughter, can start to go backwards and try to figure it out but you won't. I was present and I can't figure it out and I'm pretty smart. We can't undo this."

But to undo it is what I want. I want there to be a why. On the train to Treblinka my father saw a tiny window he could squeeze through. He jumped down into the snow. When he and Paul got to America they faced the question: What about the others? Joe tells me Sabina was angry that Paul arrived with a few family diamonds still sewn into the lining of his coat. "She had a guilt complex about leaving Poland and having almost her entire family killed. She was critical of him for not having taken care of their mother."

My father, too, may have felt judged for not saving his mother. Maybe he felt he needed to take to his heels and again run for his life.

PART III

CHAPTER 12

Driving to Treblinka

The extermination of Jews in Poland was not at all a secret: it happened in plain view of everyone, it was an absolutely public affair.
Claude Lanzmann in *Au Sujet de Shoah*

IT'S THE SORT OF EXCURSION where you find yourself hopelessly lost in the countryside northwest of Warsaw asking a couple of elderly smiling Polish farmers, "Which way to the death camp?" They look at each other. "Treblinki?" they say. "Brok!" They beam.

We've been through this little hamlet near the Bug River at least four times now. It's a picturesque enough place where storks make their huge nests on top of power poles, but there are only so many times you can watch the same scenery unspooling outside the car window on a sunny June day.

The farmers bring out a map. "Dziękuję," we say. Thank you. Against odds historic, geographic and vehicular we've come this far. There's no turning back.

It's 2010. We've arrived in Warsaw the day before to find we haven't factored into our crazy schedule—we have only a few days—a major Catholic holiday. The amplified chanting of a priest floated over Castle Square in the rebuilt Old Town and into the window of our hotel room. The whole of Warsaw was out, calling into gold-leaf-encrusted

Catholic churches then cruising the shops, every second one of which seemed to bear a sign promising Lody (ice cream) or Alkohole. We'd need a bit of the latter on this sort of trip.

It's proving almost impossible to find a way to get to the place where, nearly seventy years before, my family was murdered. Unlike Auschwitz, Treblinka isn't a major tourist destination. It is, for obvious reasons, in the middle of nowhere.

Chris volunteers to drive us there, but on a public holiday no one will rent us a car. The kind woman at our little hotel knows someone who knows someone, so we end up in a dark street late at night taking possession of a small vehicle from a man in a crumpled suit. The navigation device will no longer affix to the dashboard and, as we find when we set off, is out of date when it comes to finding death camps. At one point it directs us to a dead-end road excavation. "Treblinka?" we enquire of an old man and his dog. They look at us as if we're mad.

If the past is another country, for me that country is Poland. Jews have lived here for a thousand years. Before the Second World War they made up over a third of the population. Ninety percent of them, including close to one hundred percent of my father's family, were murdered. Half of all Jews who perished in the Holocaust were from Poland. It's where my roots are. It's a graveyard.

The only real bitterness I heard my father express was against his fellow Poles. "They wouldn't give us guns," he said of the Polish underground. Some varieties of partisans, like the Armia Krajowa, the Home Army, had a virulently anti-Semitic element who were as likely to kill Jews as Germans. The promised support for the ghetto fighters was slow to come and inadequate. Many non-Jewish Poles risked their lives and those of their families—in occupied Poland helping a Jew was a capital offence—but there were also many who hunted down and turned in Jews, looted their property, took their homes.

Meanwhile the world largely turned away. When Polish government-in-exile member Szmul Zygielbojm committed suicide in London in May 1943, he left a letter: "I cannot continue to live and to be silent while the remnants of Polish Jewry, whose representative I am, are being killed. My comrades in the Warsaw ghetto fell with arms in their hands in the last heroic battle. I was not permitted to fall like them, together with them, but I belong with them, to their mass grave. By my death, I wish to give expression to my most profound protest against the inaction in which the world watches and permits the destruction of the Jewish people." As I write, records from the United Nations War Crimes Commission that have been effectively inaccessible for more than seventy years reveal that the Allies knew as early as December 1942 about the fate of the Jews in Nazi-occupied countries and did little to prevent the slaughter.

The past won't leave Poland alone. My cousin Joe went there once on the same sort of mission we are on—chasing ghosts. "The Poles were schizoid," he wrote to me. "German occupying soldiers many times hunted Poles and sent them off to camps, and at the same time Poles hunted Jews and wanted to seize their property."

Joe's uncle Bernard, my great-uncle, who didn't survive, had a farm seized during the Nazi occupation. Joe wanted to visit it. "The current owner, a Volksdeutsche—an ethnic German living in Poland—was really very angry and would not even let me set foot on the property, threatening all sorts of violence against me. He knows he stole Bernard's property and got away with it because Bernard Jonisz was a Jew and the German occupying authorities gave him a deed." It was 1992 and a Jew was still not welcome.

I had never wanted to go to Poland. Then in 2010 Chris won a press fellowship and we ended up in the UK, living for three months at Wolfson College, Cambridge, the sort of extraordinary place where you find yourself having conversations over dinner about the use of horses in the First World War. I was content riding my bike along the river to Grantchester, the village where Rupert Brooke once lived—"And is there honey still for tea?" But Chris's study at Cambridge was partly about the architecture of murder and memorial. Architects were involved in the monuments erected to remember the Holocaust. Architects designed and engineered the machines of death. "We're going to Poland," Chris said.

We went to Kraków first. I thought I recalled my father saying he was brought up in Warsaw but born in Kraków but any documents I've found have him born in Warsaw. Maybe he lived in Kraków for a while.

Standing in the line at the airport there was a feeling of dread. I was stepping on soil where my people were hunted like animals. Going back to Poland: that's how the children of Polish survivors catch themselves describing it, even if we've never been near the place, a place in imagination full of the sepia-tinted lost. To be there is to realise the past is more dynamic and dimensional than you ever thought. In 2010 we breathed it. We stayed in Kazimierz, the district where before the war many of Kraków's over 60,000 Jewish inhabitants lived. Fewer than 6,000 survived the Holocaust. By 1978 the Jewish population could be numbered in the hundreds. Kazimierz was left to squatters, addicts, bohemians.

By the time we visit, the district has become a sort of Jewish revival theme park. Our hotel featured in the movie *Schindler's List*. It has the town's only mikveh—ritual Jewish bath—and an apparently therapeutic salt grotto in the cellar. The shops are full of dubious tchotchkes, rows of carved wooden figures of stereotypical Jews. Very popular are zydki, bearded little "lucky" Jews carrying a bag of loot, counting money, or just holding a coin. I read there's a tradition of turning your lucky Jew over on the Sabbath so their money falls out. Some take them along to football games for luck. If your team doesn't win it's the Jew's fault.

Is it nostalgia, as the sales pitch goes, or anti-Semitism? What is disturbing and mesmerising about Kazimierz is that it feels like both: sentimental yearning for a vibrant vanished culture coupled with evasion about what actually happened to all those "lucky" Jews and their money bags.

Kazimierz has Jewish restaurants, klezmer bands: everything but actual Jews. Some Jewish visitors are charmed. Others use words such as "Shtetl chic" and "Jewrassic Park". It's funny. It's grotesque. Polish Jewish journalist Konstanty Gebert put the contemporary experience of Jewish absence in Poland like this: "You cannot have genocide and then have people live as if everything is normal. It's like when you lose a limb. Poland is suffering from Jewish phantom pain."

One night we order cholent, a traditional Jewish stew, in a restaurant on Szeroka Street called, mistily, Once Upon a Time in Kazimierz. Several fashionably distressed old Jewish shops have been knocked together and decorated with evocative memorabilia. It's an example of what I come to think of as the slippage we will find everywhere in Poland. Many things related to Jews and Jewishness are just a little—or a lot—off-key.

The menu promises a "trip down memory lane" to a pre-war idyll when Jews and Gentiles lived happily together. "All barriers between them seemed to just disappear and melt away." The shop sign boards "still proudly announce their owners' names, today with their much-weathered paint and names flaking off": Stanisław Nowak, Benjamin Holcer, Szymon Kac, Chajim Kohan. "Sit down at the original carpenter's workbench," urges the menu, "touch the flywheel of an ancient sewing machine." I turn over the page to read the fate of the owners of the fading names proudly displayed outside, those who built at the bench and worked the sewing machine. Not a word. The truth wouldn't be good for the appetite.

Are the owners of the restaurant Jewish? I ask our waitress. "No," she says. There's the conversation-stopping look I will see a lot in Poland: shutters sliding down. Let's not talk about that.

I'm familiar with this. In 1968, under the guise of anti-Zionism, a campaign drove thousands of the small number of remaining Jews from the country. A beautiful coffee-table book called *Remnants: The Last Jews of Poland* came out in the 1980s, when it seemed there would soon be no Polish Jews left. I asked a Polish acquaintance about the dwindling numbers. "Oh," he said airily, "they all wanted to go live somewhere else." The look. We didn't pursue the matter.

Some of the Jewish revival is being led by Jewish organisations and by people finally connecting with their Jewish heritage, suppressed during the communist era. But this renewal runs headlong into Polish nationalism, which thrives on anti-Semitism while denying it exists. There's a sense that Polish Jews are Jews, not Poles. There's a refusal to acknowledge pogroms like those in Jedwabne in 1941 and Kielce in 1946.

While we are in Poland the *Kraków Post* runs an interview with a Polish academic, Aleksander Skotnicki, whose grandmother was killed for helping to save Jews during the Holocaust. The professor was being honoured for his work on Jewish heritage. He was asked about *Fear*, the second book by a Polish-born American academic, Jan T. Gross, on the subject of Polish wartime and post-war anti-Semitism. The book addresses the hostility and violence—including massacres like Kielce—experienced by survivors who tried to return home.

"What he says is true," Skotnicki says. But he is concerned about the book. "If it is the only source of information for a reader about Poland and Jews, then of course people will say, 'Ah, everybody was eating Jews for breakfast, lunch and dinner.'"

Gross launched *Fear* in Warsaw. *Time* magazine reported cries of "Lie!" and "Slander!" and a police presence. Gross has described his work as "a confrontation with ghosts in the consciousness of Polish society". As I write, he is under investigation by the Polish public prosecutor general, who is deciding whether to try him for damaging Poland's reputation.

In 2010 the Jewish Museum in the Old Synagogue of Kazimierz is busy. It has traces of sixteenth-century murals still visible. The nearby Remuh Synagogue also dates from the sixteenth century. We wander among the broken stones, scanning them for names. They are in Hebrew.

There is an exchange with the caretaker.

"Is there a list of names in English?"

"No."

Some of my father's large religious family would have surely prayed here. In the graveyard and the synagogue, Chris, who has a fractured Jewish heritage, puts on a yarmulke. I cry. Later he tells me that while photographing headstones that had been taken by the Nazis for roads or buildings he felt a powerful connection to something he'd always shrugged off. "If I had been here then," he found himself thinking, "these things would have happened to me."

GETTING TO AUSCHWITZ-BIRKENAU is not difficult. Kraków is a buzzing centre of increasingly popular "dark tourism". People have always done this. Pompeii has been a tourist destination for 250 years. The Capuchin Catacombs of Palermo—"The place where the living meet the dead"—offers 8,000 corpses, including some freakishly well-preserved babies. If you want to avoid places where people take inappropriate selfies, you'll never leave home.

Our hotel offers pamphlets. Touts tout tours in the streets. Go to Auschwitz, Schindler's factory or the salt mines, or take the whole package. When we are there Schindler's factory is closed. We go to Auschwitz by van with a nice driver and two other couples. Pleasantries are exchanged. No one says why they are making the journey. A video we are shown of footage taken by the Soviet liberators ensures the rest of the trip is in silence.

"You will see the industrialisation process of murder by the Nazis," my cousin Joe had written to me. "It is an education like no other." I had read about this forever, seen the documentaries, grown up with it, but there's nothing in your repertoire of responses suitable for visiting a machine of death. It starts with the familiar sign "Arbeit Macht Frei" ("Work will make you free"), proof that the Holocaust was also a calculated crime against the meaning of words. The more you look the less you understand, because a place like this defies any kind of reason.

In his account of his escape from the Warsaw Ghetto, my Great-uncle Paul wrote of "a house painter, a brutal murderer with the name A Hitler". It's preposterous. In *If This is a Man*, Italian survivor Primo Levi wrote of the absurdity of Auschwitz, the tattered, barely alive inmates made to march to an orchestra that was to Levi "the perceptible expression of its geometrical madness". He tries to break off an icicle outside the barracks window to slake his thirst and is stopped by a kapo. "Why?" he asks. "Hier ist kein warum," he is told. "Here there is no why."

Trooping through Auschwitz with thousands of other tourists sometimes feels like a ghastly parody. Block five contains "Material Evidence of Crime", heartbreaking displays behind glass of beautifully smocked baby dresses, tiny woollen hats brought along against the cold, hopefully labelled luggage. The hair, some of it carefully plaited, has faded to grey, as if it has carried on ageing in the absence of its owners.

There is a shrine to Father Kolbe, the heroic priest who volunteered to die in the starvation cells to save another prisoner. We see no tribute to any Jewish hero, such as the woman mentioned in the book *Auschwitz* by Robert Jan van Pelt and Debórah Dwork. Selected to work, she chose to go the other way. A four-year-old girl was holding her hand and she couldn't bear the child going to her death alone. I could ask about that but I don't.

More than a million people were gassed to death at Auschwitz—ninety percent of them Jews. At Birkenau we are relieved to be free to wander. The gas chambers and crematoria remain as ruins. I ask our guide what she thinks about the Jewish revival. She says, "You will have to ask someone in Kraków."

Here there is no going off script. Auschwitz has been contested ideological territory since the war, bent to the service of either Polish nationalism or communist ideology. It wasn't until 1968 that the first exclusively Jewish exhibition was mounted here, and 1989 before the genocide of the Jews was mentioned on the monument at Birkenau. There has been an attempt to site a Carmelite convent on the periphery of the camp: a battle between the Cross and the Star of David. History is always up for grabs.

While we are at Birkenau we hardly speak. I have been feeling uneasy at how long it has taken on our tour for the word "Jew" to be mentioned. "The main camp first and foremost preserved Polish—not Jewish—history," Dwork and van Pelt have written. It's at Birkenau that the enormity of the crime hits home. This place is the inevitable conclusion of the Nazis' mad industry.

Chris is troubled by the chronology of the tour. It feels like Birkenau has been relegated to a postscript. The tour, he thinks, should start at this place, with its vast modernist grid of horse barracks, now mostly reduced to crumbling chimney stacks; its ramp; its cattle wagon; the latrine barrack that once served 7,000 prisoners; the machinery of death configured so the victims could save everyone trouble by walking to their deaths. Architects designed this.

There's an argument that camps like Auschwitz-Birkenau should have been left as they were, not turned into museums and monuments. That's a difficult position to take when you see new generations walking stunned through the exhibits. It's a place to subdue even youthful exuberance, although not quite: there's something heartening about the sight of a group of teenage boys taking clandestine photos of each other in a punishment cell. "The aims of life," Levi said, "are the best defence against death."

In that spirit an Australian artist took her father, an eighty-nine-year-old survivor, to Auschwitz, where they danced to Gloria Gaynor's "I Will Survive". The old guy also danced in his "Survivor" T-shirt at other sites, including Hitler's intended "Museum of an Extinct Race" in Prague, with grandchildren the entire might of the Third Reich tried to prevent being born. That stubborn DNA. The clip is on YouTube. I watched with my daughter. "Mum," she said, "stop crying."

Some people were outraged by what they saw as dancing on graves. Yet if you were to avoid dancing where people have been murdered, there would be little dancing in Poland and many other places. As one YouTube commentator said, "Yeah, screw you, Adolf, with a gay anthem made famous by a black woman. Respect comes in many forms."

IN LILY BRETT'S NOVEL *Too Many Men*, Ruth takes her survivor father Edek back to Poland. "There is nothing there," Edek says. "We are visiting one nothing after another." I think of that as, back in Warsaw, we tramp over kilometres of the city, trying to trace the remains of the ghetto. It is easy to miss a stone here, a marking on the pavement there. The ghetto was destroyed after the 1943 uprising, during which the starving remnants of Warsaw's Jewish population held off the Germans for more than a month. We pay our respects at Nathan Rapoport's bleak monument *Warsaw Ghetto Uprising*, unveiled in 1948. Heroes of the uprising stand staunchly on one side. Around the back a line of victims, mostly women and children, walk to their deaths. One child, holding the hand of an elderly woman, turns to meet the eye of the viewer. There is a stall selling memorabilia. Desperate for something tangible to hold on to out of this tour of gaps and absences I buy a book, which the seller stamps with place and date.

The ghetto took most of 1940 to be built. It was sealed off on November 16. From July 22 to September 21, 1942, 300,000 Jews were deported, my family among them. Sixty thousand remained. In January 1943 there was a second wave of deportations. In April, as the final liquidation of the ghetto began, so did the uprising. A month later the liquidation was complete.

Władislaw Szpilman, whose book about his survival in Warsaw became Roman Polanski's movie *The Pianist*, writes of meeting a friend just before an "action" in the ghetto to take people for deportation. His friend says, "'You wait, it'll all be over some fine day, because'… and he waved his arms about… 'because there isn't any sense in it, is there?'"

It's impossible to imagine it, presumptuous to try.

But there are echoes. My father's memory: "You would wake up and the person next to you is dead." My Great-aunt Faiga's last desperate message. Szpilman's observations of the Lithuanian and Ukrainian fascists brought in to help deport Jews from the ghetto: "They liked killing anyway… They killed children before their mothers' eyes and found the women's despair amusing."

I remember my father talking about the cruelty of the Ukrainians. "They were worse than the Germans," he said. These fragments he shared were coded messages I'm still trying to crack years later through reading the accounts of other survivors and the diaries of those who didn't survive. Oh, I think, so that's what he was trying to tell me about. That's what he saw. That is what he lived through.

We go to the Umschlagplatz, the holding area at the northern edge of the ghetto from which Jews were sent to Treblinka. In his diary for September 5, 1942, Abraham Lewin recorded the scenes as people were concentrated into ever smaller areas to await deportation. "A sight that I will never forget as long as I live. Five tiny children,

Umschlagplatz, the holding area next to the railway station in Warsaw from which more than 300,000 Jews were sent to their deaths in the Treblinka camp from 1942–43.

two- and three-year-olds, sit on a camp bed in the open from Monday to Tuesday and cry and cry and scream without stopping—'Mummy, mummy, I want to eat.' The soldiers are shooting continually and the shots silence the children for a moment. The children lay there for 24 hours, sobbing and screaming, 'Mummy, mummy.' Tuesday afternoon a middle-aged man, aged about 50, went up to them, broke down into a continual, choking sobbing and gave the children a little something to eat. Earlier, women had come up and given them food. Our hearts have turned to stone and there was no way to save them. What are we saving them for if we are all sentenced to die?"

Lewin's wife Luba has already been deported. He is sent to Treblinka with his fifteen-year-old daughter Ora.

At the Umschlagplatz we have to negotiate our way around an Israeli tour group that has taken over the monument. I feel irrationally annoyed. At most other places, like the fragment of ghetto wall we

Women and children being deported to Treblinka from the Siedlice Ghetto, ninety miles from Warsaw.

had to creep through private property to get to, we have been alone. We could have taken a tour but, after the organisation of Auschwitz, visiting the Umschlagplatz was something we wanted to do—in our bumbling shell-shocked way—on our own.

0   100   200 km

BALTIC SEA

LATVIA

LITHUANIA

• Wilno

Danzig

EAST PRUSSIA
(Germany)

Neman

■ Chelmno

Brok   Małkinia
        ■ Treblinka
Poznań   Urle
        Warsaw •   • Siedlce
Warta
        • Łódź   • Żelechów, Garwolin County

        GERMANY   ■ Sobibór
                Lublin • ■ Majdanek

                Wista   Bug

                        ■ Bełżec

        • Kraków   SOVIET
Auschwitz-Birkenau   • Lwów   UNION

CZECHOSLOVAKIA

■ Extermination camp
   General Government
   Territory annexed to Germany
   Territory adminstered by Germany

HUNGARY

ROMANIA

POLAND, 1942/43. Germany invaded Poland on September 1, 1939, starting
the war in Europe. On September 17 the Soviet Union invaded from the
east. Warsaw surrendered on September 27 and the Polish government fled
into exile through Romania. Germany and the Soviet Union then divided
the country between them, but in the summer of 1941 the Soviet forces were
driven out by the Germans' Operation Barbarossa. General Government
was the German administrative centre.

WE HAVE FURTHER OCCASION TO RETHINK this independent strategy while driving to Treblinka. Getting lost aside, the trip has become increasingly grim. The road goes for miles through ancient forest where Polish and Jewish partisans hid, the sort of place where my father must have hidden.

There are two camps. Treblinka I is the work camp, which we won't have time to visit. We arrive at Treblinka II, the extermination camp. It is not one of the well-known camps. No one was liberated here. My father once said there were worse places than Auschwitz. This is the place he meant.

Treblinka, built in 1942 and one of the Operation Reinhard camps, along with Bełżec and Sobibór, was designed solely for the killing of Jews. People were dragged half dead from the boxcars, made to undress, driven with whips down the "Himmelstrasse" ("Road to Heaven") and thrown into gas chambers, often within two hours. Guards were allowed to grab babies and smash their heads on the boxcars. The sick were taken to the Lazarette (infirmary) and shot at the edge of a pit. According to the United States Holocaust Memorial Museum, from July 1942 through November 1943, between 870,000 and 925,000 Jews were murdered at Treblinka.

In Claude Lanzmann's nine-and-a-half-hour film *Shoah* he covertly interviews Franz Suchomel, who was an SS officer at Treblinka. No one who has seen the film can forget seeing Suchomel sing the Treblinka song. Lanzmann ensures this by making him sing it twice, "But loud!"

All that matters now is Treblinka.
It is our destiny.
That's why we've become one with Treblinka
in no time at all.

Memorial of granite rocks at the site of the Treblinka camp. It's been estimated as many as 900,000 Jews were murdered here between July 1942 and August 1943.

Suchomel describes the arrival of trains like the one my father jumped from. "The windows were closed off with barbed wire so no one could get out. On the roofs were the 'hellhounds', the Ukrainians or Latvians…" My father, who knew by then that the only choice for a Jew in Poland was different varieties of dead, said, "I rolled down the bank and waited to be shot."

Samuel Rajzman, the only survivor to testify about Treblinka at the Nuremberg trials, outlined the process. "All those who were driven from the cars were divided into groups—men, children, and women, all separate. They were all forced to strip immediately, and this procedure continued under the lashes of the German guards' whips. Workers who were employed in this operation immediately picked up all the clothes and carried them away to barracks. Then the people were obliged to walk naked through the street to the gas chambers."

Treblinka was so busy that sometimes victims had to wait for a day or two before they were gassed. "Many knew," Suchomel says. "The men were killed first. The women had to wait ... sixty women with children ... Naked! In summer and winter." There were women who slashed their daughters' wrists at night, then cut their own. Others poisoned themselves.

There is much worse in this man's avid account than I can bring myself to write down. It's not for me to put such nightmares in anyone else's head. Suchomel insisted that Lanzmann preserve his anonymity. Lanzmann agreed. He lied.

The Germans had enough awareness to realise they might not be applauded for this work. From the mass graves of the Einsatzgruppen death squads in the Soviet Union and the Baltic states, where the ground was sometimes reported to heave for days with the movements of those buried alive, to the misery and disease of the ghettos, to the bodies piled up like cord wood in the concentration camps, the more they tried to pursue their mad ideology of racial purity the more hideous a mess they made.

When SS leader Heinrich Himmler visited Treblinka in early 1943 he ordered the putrefying bodies in mass graves to be dug up and burned on grates to get rid of the evidence. Everything here now is symbolic: symbolic entrance; symbolic railway tracks; symbolic ramp to mark where victims, those still alive, disembarked. Designers have also been set the task of creating a symbolic pit, a surreal blackened river of melted basalt where the cremation pyres once burned.

The day we visit, the scene is serene and full of birdsong. There are no crowds until buses of Israeli Defense Forces personnel arrive and take over the central monument for a service. My family was here, I want to say. But I don't. Few of these young soldiers would have families untouched by what went on at places like this.

Here you can confront the how, but there are still no answers as

Photographs of Polish Jews before the Holocaust, displayed on buildings in Próżna Street, Warsaw, part of an art project And I Still See Their Faces, *begun in 1996.*

to the why. In 1970 journalist Gitta Sereny interviewed Franz Stangl in prison. He was commandant of the Treblinka extermination camp in 1942. She pressed him on how he saw his victims.

"You didn't think they were human beings?"

"Cargo," he said tonelessly. "They were cargo."

As late as 1957 sun-bleached bones and skulls poked through the ground. Apparently bone fragments can still be seen, especially after rain, but the site seems to have been tamed.

As with many Holocaust memorials we see, it's about rocks, chunks of granite that can be read like headstones but are jagged and elemental. I seek out the stone marked "Polska". "They destroyed this beautiful family, beautiful people," Joe had said. "You go to Treblinka, there are no graves. There are symbols of stone but they simply represent the dust. That's what the Germans accomplished."

Some children of survivors will not allow their feet to touch the ground here, but I have to fight a primitive urge to lie down and get as close as possible to the dust of the dead. These places make you a little crazy. There is almost no record of my family who died in Poland but at least at Treblinka, in the visitors' book in the little museum, I can write: "In memory of the Wichtel and Jonisz families who were murdered here." Outside, we place stones in the Jewish tradition, and on a memorial I leave a piece of paper listing our family's names. The rain will soon wash them away.

IN WARSAW, AT THE END OF OUR DAY walking around what was once the ghetto, we nearly don't make it to the last street, Próżna. Time is running out but the decaying tenements are easy to spot by the huge, unbearably poignant photographs on the walls of the people who once lived there and throughout Poland: families, children, old people, babies in prams. The photographs are part of a project, *And I Still See Their Faces*, created by Gołda Tencer, a Polish actress with Jewish origins. By the time we return in 2015, the area will have been tidied up and the photographs removed so the buildings can be restored, but in 2010 the buildings are still as they were when my father was here. We peer through broken windows and into eerie inner courtyards, unable to stop looking for ghosts.

At street level a small bar tunnels into a near-ruined building, the weight of history bearing down upon it. Outside, a young Jewish guy in a yarmulke sits drinking with friends. He looks like he feels at home. I'm not sure how at home I can ever feel in Poland but it's the place where fragments of my family remain, and where the history of what happened to them is still being debated, evaded, prodded and played out. Even the slippage and the evasion are testament to the power of what happened here—an answer to those who say these events never happened and I just somehow mislaid more than a hundred members of my extended family. Poland is as close as I'm going to get to them. Before we leave, I will know I want to come back.

Meanwhile, we badly need a drink. The girl at the bar in Próżna Street casts a cool eye over two tired and dusty dark tourists.

"Yes?"

"Do you have wine?"

"No."

We have vodka.

CHAPTER 13

Stolpersteine and stelae

To forget the dead would be akin to killing them a second time.

Elie Wiesel in *Night*

BERLIN IS MODERN, DIVERSE, and seems to be meeting its history head-on, at least on the level of the built environment. It's unnerving, in 2010, to feel more comfortable here than in Poland. My father always had German friends, something my mother could never understand.

In a city of memorials, you walk alongside the dead. One of the most moving of these memorials, a project initiated by German artist Gunter Demnig, requires you to keep your eyes open and look down not up. The Stolpersteine (stumbling stones) are small brass plaques set into the pavement and inscribed with the names of individual victims of the Nazis at the site of their last place of residence: history designed to trip you up. The inscriptions we find outside a building near our hotel tell us that here lived Herman and Jenny Schneebaum and their children Thea, 12, and Victor, 2. They were deported to Auschwitz in 1943. "Ermordet": murdered.

The project has spread to other countries. In Poland permission was given, then withdrawn. By 2016 a few Stolpersteine will have been allowed in some towns. Maybe one day we will place one in Praga.

Berlin's Memorial to the Murdered Jews of Europe is easier to find.

You can't miss it. A city block is covered with 2,711 concrete slabs, or stelae, arranged in a grid pattern but slightly askew. Walking through them on the undulating ground in single file, as you must, you feel you could be swallowed up. The young, unable to resist the challenge, ignore the sign forbidding jumping from stone to stone.

Designed by New York architect Peter Eisenman, the memorial, approved in 1999 after much controversy, opened in 2004. There were objections not just to Eisenman's abstract and enigmatic design but to the idea of a memorial at all. Martin Waiser, a novelist, demanded to know in what other country in the world there was "a memorial of national ignominy" smack in the middle of a capital city. Björn Höcke, a senior member of the populist Alternative for Germany Party, has recently echoed this, pronouncing: "Germans are the only people in the world who plant a monument of shame in the heart of the capital."

Others have objected that the monument is too discreet. There's no sign to tell you what it is. The words "Holocaust" or "Shoah" don't appear in the name. The entrance to the information centre, which presents the histories of lost families, their names and their words, is not immediately obvious. It's architecture that forces you to ask questions.

Entering this subterranean centre will see a low point in our careers as dark tourists. It begins when we visit Checkpoint Charlie, site of the Cold War border crossing between East and West Germany. Just as Poland has its unnerving nostalgia for the Jews, in Germany there's a yearning for the culture associated with the German Democratic Republic that vanished with the fall of the wall in 1989.

There is an element of high kitsch about GDR-themed Berlin tourist attractions. At Checkpoint Charlie, Chris, who almost never buys mementos, is drawn to a souvenir gas mask. Go on, I say magnanimously.

He buys the gas mask and puts it his backpack. We forget all about it until we walk down the stairs to the information centre. Coming from our part of the world we have forgotten that, as in many public places in Europe—and just about all public places where things Jewish are involved—our bags will be X-rayed. We've handed them over before we realise we are bringing a gas mask into a Holocaust museum. It's too late to grab back the bag and run out.

Events seem to unfold in slow motion.

"What," the guard says, holding the offending object between thumb and index finger, "is this?"

"A souvenir gas mask?" Chris quavers.

The guard rolls his eyes. The gas mask is confiscated. When we leave, the guard hands it back with a withering look. It occurs to us how many airport X-ray machines there are between us and home. Chris bins the mask. This is the nearest we get to an inadvertent Holocaust joke.

Jews have reserved the right to be funny about the Holocaust. It was a revelation in the '90s to see New Zealand comedian Deb Filler's one-woman show *Punch Me in the Stomach*, about her survivor father Saul Filler. My father had uttered the same words. Were all survivor fathers proud of their abs?

Deb accompanies her father on a tour of the death camps of Eastern Europe. At Auschwitz she needs to go to the toilet. "Well, don't be too long," Saul says. "I got locked in here once before. I don't want to get locked in again."

The exiled German Jewish philosopher Theodor Adorno famously said there could be no poetry after Auschwitz. There could, it seems, be comic books, including Art Spiegelman's graphic telling of his father's story, *Maus*. In 1940 in Gurs, an internment camp in south-west France, Horst Rosenthal made a booklet entitled *Mickey Mouse in Gurs*, using Mickey as a stand-in for himself. "I have no papers," Mickey explains to a gendarme. "I'm international."

Rosenthal was murdered at Auschwitz.

Jews being marched to the Umschlagplatz for deportation to Treblinka after the Warsaw Ghetto uprising that began in April 1943. Although German soldiers set fire to the ghetto building by building, pockets of resistance continued for almost a month.

Jerry Seinfeld wondered whether it was all right to make out while watching *Schindler's List*. My father wanted us to laugh at his stories of fooling young German soldiers in the Polish forest. The doomed historian and archivist Emanuel Ringelblum took the time to record ghetto jokes in his remarkable journal. In one a police chief comes to the apartment of a woman to take away her belongings. She pleads that she is a widow with a child. He says he will take nothing if she can guess which of his eyes is the artificial one.

She guesses the left. The police chief asks her how she knew. "Because that one has a human look," she answers.

Mostly, though, there aren't a lot of laughs for the dark tourist in Berlin. Memorials are everywhere, not only to Jews but to others murdered by the Third Reich: homosexuals, Sinti and Roma, the disabled. No amount of memorials explains why, in living memory, the people of a civilised European culture colluded in first the persecution and then the mass slaughter of their friends, colleagues and neighbours.

During the Warsaw Ghetto uprising, as buildings burned and people held off the Germans, the Catholic newspaper *Prawda Młodych* (*Young People's Truth*) saw an opportunity for Jewish redemption. "Prayer for those being killed, making them aware that their present suffering may constitute a great sacrificial pyre bringing swifter renewal, removing the curse from a nation that was once the chosen people... Their souls will be cleansed and redeemed by the baptism of blood, equally important and holy as the baptism of water." Any reason will do, or no reason.

WE STAY IN A LITTLE PENSION in one of Berlin's "gayborhoods" run by a Polish woman who mothers us and clucks over our inability to make much impression on her breakfasts of boiled eggs, cold meats, breads and cheeses. One day we take a trip to Bad Arolsen to visit ITS, the International Tracing Service. ITS began in 1943 as a registration and tracing service for missing persons.

To get to Bad Arolsen takes six hours on a train, return. This is ambitious, even by our standards. But after one nothing after another, here there is something. The place is the world's largest Nazi archive, holding more than thirty million documents about the fate of seventeen and a half million people, the scrupulously detailed paperwork of the Third Reich. It includes documents relating to forced labour used by German churches and businesses. For decades the archives were restricted on the ground of privacy. When we visit they have been fully open for only two years.

Here you can study the vocabulary of mass murder. "The load should be nine to 10 per square metres," reads a letter about the requirements for trucks used to kill the disabled. The load. We see a concentration camp lice control card: each prisoner is listed, along with the number of lice found. There's a camp death book recording the killing of prisoners at two-minute intervals over an hour and a half. "Look at the date," archivist Udo Jost says of one entry, "April 20, 1942. The birthday of Adolf Hitler and they make a present to the Führer."

I know there will be little evidence of my family among these records. My cousin Joe applied for information in the 1980s and found nothing. There was no registering of those who were sent to Treblinka, no numbers or names. But at the end of our visit some staff members come to speak to me. They move in close, bring a box of tissues. Two documents have been found. One is a list in French of survivors in Poland. It includes "Wichtel, Benjamin, à Varsovie."

The other document, compiled by the Jewish Telegraphic Agency, contains the names of survivors who have been put in touch with relatives in America. On one side is listed "Wichtel, Benjamin from Warsaw." On the other: "Wichtel, A.S., New York, N.Y." The list is dated September 1944. Uncle Sy has found his brother.

CHAPTER 14

Uncle Paul

"I know you. You are a Jew and let's go."
Uncle Paul's account of a life in hiding

AT JOE'S URGING, PAUL JONISZ (Janish once he got to America) wrote his wartime story. The original in his baroque old-world hand is with other family material at the Holocaust Memorial Museum in Washington, D.C. Some of the story is written in English, inflected with Polish and Yiddish. The parts written in Polish have been translated and summarised by the museum.

The documents I receive, Notebook One and Notebook Two, are a mix of Paul's words and the translator's. Paul tells his story in the cool manner I have come to recognise from the accounts of many survivors.

"I am born in Warsaw City, which is known as a beautiful city situated on the large river Vistula. My father was very well known because of his import business in grain and vegetables in freight wagons." This was my great-grandfather Yankel Jonisz, who did well by supplying the military.

"[He] obtained a good and honest name. As a result, my father receives a gold medal from the existing government." The Jonisz pride is there in Paul's voice, even on the page: a successful man; a good and honest name. It's the same family pride I hear on the phone whenever

I speak to Joe, the pride I heard the night Uncle Sy called at two a.m. and said, "Never forget you are a Wichtel." It was in my father's voice when he spoke of his successful brother: "He has a mansion. They will spoil you rotten."

To a child's ear all that pride sounded a little boastful. I had a New Zealand mother. To her it wasn't done to big-note. Now there's a different way to hear it. Successful, honest, recipient of a gold medal: see, we were good and useful citizens. What did we do to deserve to be destroyed?

Paul, ten years older than my father, studied bookkeeping and on a course met his future wife, seventeen-year-old Barbara. Her Polish name was Bronisława, Bronka for short. "We used to be always together since our mentality was different from the rest of our families," Paul writes, hinting at tensions. Maybe it wasn't just the war that kept those who survived from cohering as a family.

At twenty-one Paul was in the Polish army. Barbara's parents won a lottery and moved to Germany. Paul followed and studied in Hamburg. Two years later he returned to Warsaw. Even in 1925 German Jews were experiencing the beginning of the end. Hitler's *Mein Kampf* was published that year. The Nazi Party began to build a mass movement. "Bad consequences from [Hitler's] propaganda," is the way Paul puts it. "Hitler started his brutal job." Barbara's parents soon returned to Warsaw as well.

Paul and Barbara bumped into each other at the movies. Reunited. "Our joy was wonderful." They married in a private ceremony in Barbara's parents' apartment. There's no talk of his orthodox Jonisz family being invited.

The couple's happiness was short-lived, thanks to the "housepainter, a brutal murderer with the name A Hitler". On September 1, 1939 the war against Poland began. "We didn't expect his murder plan so quickly."

Paul and Barbara, living in a beautiful five-room apartment on the corner of Marszałkowska and Wilcza Streets, knew what was happening to Jews in Germany. Soon in Warsaw "the SS men came to Jewish apartments with whips". Jews were dragged from their homes and made to work, repairing utilities damaged by the German attackers. Paul will not write about the Holocaust in general: he knows many books have already been written. "But I like to mention that Poles believed … the hate was against the Jews only, making a big mistake by not helping enough with weapons, food and medication."

The situation worsened with shocking suddenness. Ghettos were built, announcements made. "All Jews must move from their apartments to the ghetto … Every Jew must wear a band with the Jewish symbol. Under these circumstances the Jews realised how tragic the situation is, and their fate is doomed." Some escaped to Russia. Paul doesn't say why he didn't try to escape. Maybe Barbara wouldn't leave her parents.

He and Barbara moved to a small apartment in the ghetto. Barbara was secretary for women in the ghetto's third section. Paul became chairman of a section of ZTOS, an activist organisation to help the poor and sick. These self-help bodies, and others like CENTOS for the care of orphans, were organised by, among others, Emanuel Ringelblum, the historian and politician known for his *Notes from the Warsaw Ghetto*, the journal he kept secretly to record the mounting horror. These activist groups operated behind the façade of official organisations. Hundreds worked for them. The salary: a bowl of soup.

Paul mentions none of his Jonisz family, although by the end of August 1941 his mother Brandla has died of starvation and been buried at the Jewish Cemetery in Okopowa Street. The translator records: "Paul writes that he was unable to find out what exactly happened to his large family and to his wife's family."

By this time Paul and my father will have known what was happening to Jews in other parts of Poland—the massacres by the

Einsatzgruppen, the SS paramilitary death squads. As recorded in the book *Who Will Write Our History?* about Emanuel Ringelblum, by late January 1942 farewell letters were arriving in the ghetto from Jews about to be deported from other places. One contained an ominous coded message about Treblinka: "Uncle [the Nazis] was building a new house very near to you."

In late March and early April the Warsaw Ghetto underground learned of the plan for total extermination and began to plan armed resistance. My father said he was in the underground. It was on April 23 that the head of the Judenrat, Adam Czerniaków, refused to sign orders to deport children. For Paul the memory is still bitter. "Czerniaków returning home commits the same day suicide. … not one voice was to hear from still free Europe and USA in order to help the growing tragic situation of the Jews in Germany and Poland. The USA, British or French could have bombed the gas chambers in concentration camps and saved millions of innocent people!"

Until I found my cousin Joe in 2006, I had thought it was Paul who had jumped from the train with my father. I learned it was another man, identity unknown. The section of Paul's diary translated from Polish tells of his own escape, beginning with the day his street was blockaded. All the inhabitants of the apartments had to come down to the street. Here a selection was made. Men and women were separated, children and parents.

"Paul, standing among the men, was sure he is sentenced to death," the summary says. He is thirty-nine, fit, well dressed. Each man has to pass the head of the Gestapo and his entourage. "When Paul passed by the master of life and death, he pushed him with his horsewhip towards the group going to the death camp." Barbara, not among the women selected, bribed a Jewish policeman with a gold coin, got a white doctor's coat and managed to pass it to Paul. He put it on and strolled away. Walk, don't run.

On September 21, 1942 the couple's luck ran out. Their house at 24 Nowolipie Street was surrounded by SS, gendarmes and Ukrainian units. Paul and others barricaded themselves behind a wardrobe. Germans and Ukrainians entered the apartment and took things, including items from the wardrobe, but miraculously failed to discover the door behind it.

After a few hours it seemed the "action" was finished. "A neighbour told Bronka that all is over and she should cross the street to the other side where it's safer. The very moment Bronka stepped out she was stopped by a Jewish policeman."

Paul rushed over with a bribe but it didn't work. There was a fight. "My wife was kidnapped by a Jewish policeman—which I almost killed—and he called in two Ukrainians with two rifles and they took me by force and kept me several hours on the wall of a building. The Ukrainians saw my gold watch which they took away by force including my gold chain." At that moment Paul saw his wife shot.

Joe fills in the story. "Paul's wife Barbara was ordered for 'resettlement'. When she failed to report, the Kapos—Jewish Police—came to the apartment in the ghetto and dragged [her] out on to the street. She was screaming so she was shot by an SS guard in front of Paul. That made him determined to escape."

Put into a slave labour gang, Paul looks for an opportunity to escape. He has managed to hide some gold coins and a diamond in the thick soles of his shoes. As his group of labourers marches on Leszno Street towards Żelazna Street, he takes his chance. "It was dark, late in the evening. I got a good place to run from the group."

He goes to the house of a friend, Dr Leszczyński. "[He] asked about my wife Bronisława and after the tragic news became very upset." On the street again he has to bribe two Polish men who guess he has escaped from the ghetto and threaten to take him to the Gestapo. In the end he gives the men money he had hidden in his hat. He begs for a little back for a tram ride. They give him twenty złoty and leave him alone.

Joe has told me Paul was the member of the family most likely to pass as gentile. He wasn't religious. He'd studied in Germany and spoke the language. He used the more Polish-sounding name Paweł Janiszewski. But his account makes clear that betrayal was an ever-present threat.

He sleeps on mattresses in damp basements. At one point he goes to the superintendent of his old apartment on Wilcza Street. "The super came out and started to cry. 'Mr Paul, you are alive.'" He is given a room in the building by a woman who believes he is a Polish officer in hiding from the Nazis. He has a hiding place he gets to by crawling through the doors of a sideboard. "This small niche in a large room performed the most important role in my life on the other side." The superintendent, Mr Władysław, is accused of hiding Jews and tortured by the Gestapo for two weeks but gives no one away. Someone gives Paul work making lace.

With the ghetto uprising finally crushed, the Nazis turn their attention to Poles. "Doctors, engineers, and professors started to disappear without any information about what was happening to them. ... It wasn't Jews anymore and the kidnapping of Poles from the streets and apartments was a daily job for the Nazis."

He has a succession of close calls. Looking into a shop window he notices a man following him. He moves away. "He moves also right after me, crying loud… 'I know you. You are a Jew and let's go.' I was young and still able to take action so I hit him with my heavy bundle right in his face and he lost the eyeglasses and fell on the street … I took a cab and ran quick to a coffee shop under the Domański Restaurant, resting about two hours."

There is another scrape as he travels to deliver lace to salesmen. "Two hoods probably recognised me that I must be Jewish [although]

I was well dressed with dark glasses and a Polish moustache." He forces himself on to a crowded tram. "But one hood ran after me in the back and the other was hanging in the front on the stairs … I made a big noise that a robber was after me and this caused a panic in the tram. I was moving fast forward and came to the guy in the front. Again with a big blow to the face he ran away." He gets off at the next stop, takes a three-seat bicycle, and goes into a restaurant, "resting there for several hours".

By now looking like a Pole is not much help. During one round-up he takes a risk and ducks into a Germans-only café. "[I] took inside a German newspaper and ordered a sandwich, soup and beer. After 2½ hours the kidnapping was over and I was able to reach my location."

He witnesses the 1944 Warsaw Uprising. From August 1 to October 2, with the Russians approaching, the Polish resistance forces fight to try and liberate Warsaw from the Germans: "Every building was a funeral home and no help from the Red Army." The roof of the house in Wilcza Street catches alight. "I was in charge and ordered the tenants to get pails with water from the street … We were able to save the building."

The Jews fight courageously, finally evoking back-handed affirmation from their fellow Poles. A report in the underground press sees the fighting as "in no way the reaction of victims defending themselves but … undoubtedly a conscious act of will, carried out in the name of human honour and dignity. For this reason … the fighters of the Warsaw Ghetto should be awarded full respect and support."

When the uprising is finally crushed, Poles are given twenty-four hours to get out of the city. "Big columns of people without to see an end. One gestapo with a strong whip attacked a priest, crying 'Arbeiten!' You must work. The blood began to flow from the priest's face … and he fell down on the street." Paul tells the Gestapo in German that the priest has been working a few blocks away. "The Gestapo stopped the beating ... I saved the life of this priest."

Paul and a few other men take the opportunity to escape again. He knows a man in a nearby repair shop and the SS don't see them walking down the hill towards it. From the window he watches the "colossal columns of people"; they remind him of "the thousands of Jews—men, women and children in the Warsaw Ghetto—[who] went without resistance to concentration camps to die in gas chambers." The shop owner feeds them for a fee, then gets them a horse and cart. Paul ends up in Opacz, a village twenty kilometres from Warsaw, where he hides in a barn during searches.

The Red Army will finally liberate Warsaw on January 17, 1945.

AFTER THE WAR PAUL, like my father, went back to Warsaw. "He writes that he felt like an ancient man," says the translator of his diary, "completely exhausted by the experiences of the previous six years, death of his wife and the rest of his family."

Jews didn't always receive a warm welcome. Paul found his wartime business partner, who owed him money. "Wróbel expressed surprise that he was still alive and claimed he didn't owe him any money. In addition, he didn't say a word about the death of Paul's wife and her whole family, which Wróbel knew for many years. Finally Wróbel paid a few gold 10 ruble coins, which was a small part of what he owed."

Paul went to Łódź, where he opened a textile factory. He returned to his old apartment on Wilcza Street on weekends but became ill and depressed. What was there in Poland for him?

"Many Jews started to think of emigration. Paul received a telegram from his nephew from the US, who found out he was alive. He started to think of immigration to the US. Life in a communist country looked less and less attractive. Private initiative in Poland was crushed by the new government and Paul didn't want to live in such a country.

Benjamin Wichtel (left) and his uncle, Paul Jonisz, sometime between February 1946 and September 1947.

In mid 1946 Paul liquidated all his businesses in Poland and left it forever. He considered his survival a miracle, never to be forgotten."

After the war Paul reunited with my father, and they were sent to Sweden to recuperate. I have a photograph of them sitting close together, beaming. It's a proper studio portrait. Perhaps they wanted to document their continued existence with something more than a snapshot.

I've only just noticed that in the photo my father is wearing a thick gold ring with a single gem on the little finger of his left hand. I remember that ring. He told me it was from before the war. He never wore it in Canada: it lived in my mother's jewellery box.

He also had an embossed gold watch that he sometimes let us look at, with a back that opened so you could see the precise movements of its mechanism. I remember being told it had belonged to his father. By the time we left Canada, grief and bad luck had achieved what Hitler couldn't and the ring and the watch were pawned.

Paul's account ends: "As the only survivor of my and my wife's families, in hiding on the Aryan side, I constantly repeated that the world will never forget and never forgive the Germans for what they did to us." There is no mention of my father or Dora. Was this deliberate? In *Maus*, Art Spiegelman tells the story of his father Vladek Speigelman, who had to pay a cousin to help him. "You don't understand," Vladek tells his son. "At that time there wasn't anymore families. It was everybody to take care for himself."

After all Paul and my father had endured, together and apart, they had not stayed in touch. They had not remained friends. I had danced with Paul at Jerry's bar mitzvah without really understanding I was dancing with a miracle, the uncle of another miracle. Paul died in New York in 1993. On our visit there in 1990 someone told me he was far too mentally unwell to be visited. I should have written to him. I should have gone to see him.

Uncle Paul, you were a mensch. May your memory be a blessing.

CHAPTER 15

On the rocks

He stated he was frightened and persecuted all his life.
Clinical record, Brockville Psychiatric Hospital, May 1967

ON MAY 23, 1967, the police found my father wandering the streets in Cornwall on the St Lawrence River, Canada's easternmost city, trying to cross the international bridge into the United States. He must have been making one last trip to ask Sy for help. Maybe, nearly three years after we left, he was going to look for us at the mansion in New Jersey where we'd been together for Jerry's bar mitzvah, where he'd gone earlier, running through the house calling our names. On the Medical Practitioner's Certificate for the Admission of a Mentally Ill Patient he is listed as Benjamin Wetchell: "Appearance: Melancholy."

Clinical notes: "Patient stated he went 'on the rocks' two years ago when he went bankrupt." Two years ago: 1965. We were in New Zealand. Does that mean that until he went "on the rocks" he was still planning to come and join us?

WHEN MY FATHER'S FILE arrived from the Archives of Ontario in March 2015 I began to understand the silences and secrets in many families. But silence was no longer an option. As my daughter and my niece had said, "You cannot not know where your father is."

I redoubled efforts to find him, firing off emails in all directions, possibly sounding completely mad. I am still doing this. "Hello. I'm a complete stranger from the ends of the Earth. I wonder if there is anyone there who might remember my father?" I can't seem to stop.

We knew he had died in a mental institution in Canada. From the dusty attic of memory I retrieve a possible location: my mother, I'm sure, had mentioned Ontario. But both Jeff and I have tried Ontario before, looking for his death certificate. There wasn't one. Jeff had tried Quebec—Dad had spent time in Montreal—and British Columbia, just in case.

How can there be no death certificate? We were sending off for one nothing after another. Someone told me that in the old days the bodies of psychiatric patients without families were sometimes sent for medical research. Or they were just buried in unmarked graves. That would be right. Our family has form when it comes to unmarked graves.

Chris's brother-in-law Jim had been researching the Byzantine complexities of Chris's family and also quietly making some enquiries, employing his lawyer's mind and forensic research skills on behalf of my family. He suggested trying the Archives of Ontario.

"We don't get many enquiries from New Zealand," wrote the very nice French Canadian woman at the archives, as if she'd just had an access-to-information request from Mars. She came back asking for the names of my father's parents and any siblings. She came back again, asking for Uncle Sy's dates of birth and death. It was beginning to seem as though she was on to something. I didn't dare ask. I didn't dare hope.

The archives don't normally inform you by email of the outcome of a search: you either get a letter in the mail or you don't. The archivist emailed. She had found my father. Something was in the mail.

I expected a letter, a few index cards. The information took two weeks to arrive. I walked around in a state of suspended being, barely breathing. On the day it came I missed a text from Chris: "Package from Canada on dining room table." He couldn't understand why I was dawdling home while he was sitting staring at this unexploded ordnance from the past. I finally read his text while waiting for the ferry. "Wasn't going to have wine," I texted, "but am now."

The file, frayed en route, was erupting from the envelope. One hundred and fifty-eight pages: an agonising account of a life on the rocks. Clinical records, medical tests, notes from his social worker and his doctors that lurched from professional to compassionate to wits' end. One page from a nursing home to which he'd been sent read in its exasperated entirety: "This man simply cannot continue to stay here." From May 26, 1967 until his death on November 26, 1970, except for about three months when he was unleashing havoc at the Lapalme Nursing Home in Embrun, Ontario, my father had been in a psychiatric hospital. Once again he had been, in the bland designation given to him after he was liberated, a displaced person. A misplaced person. Lost. He was buried on November 30, my birthday.

I sent copies of the file to my sister Ros and my nephew Karl. I sent a copy to my brother Jeff, his wife Maureen, and his daughter Jocelyn. Chris read it. My daughter and I read it together, weeping. Our boys, the two Bens, read it. My niece Nicola, Jeff's younger daughter, read it at our house and, always cool-headed in a tight corner, pointed out things I'd missed.

You miss what you need to miss.

BROCKVILLE: IT'S A LITTLE TOWN in the Thousand Lakes region of Eastern Ontario, a four-hour drive from Toronto, where my father's last address is recorded. He had been living in Toronto for a while. His last listed job before he became too unwell to work was, he told the doctors at the psychiatric hospital, at Gabrielle Auto Company, a

The former Brockville Psychiatric Hospital, Ontario, Canada, 2015.

business of which I can find no record. We children never knew that. I don't know if my mother did.

The locals referred to the hospital as the Psych. It opened in 1894 as the Eastern Hospital for the Insane, and when we go there the abandoned Victorian building will look precisely like something with a name like that.

After decades of having nothing, I have my father's post-mortem. "External marks of violence: 1) large ecchymosis [bruise] of the right temporal and periorbital area; 2) right subconjunctival haemorrhage; 3) abrasions to right wrist, elbow and lateral thoracic wall."

He had fallen over before he died. On other occasions, he had been attacked by other patients, their names redacted in the file. October 9, 1967: [X] pushed him to the floor Monday evening. [X] admits this upon questioning." February 1970: "Hit on side of face by patient [Y]."

When he was picked up in Cornwall in May 1967, he had four suits, a topcoat, one pair of briefs. He had the suspenders and armbands I remember him always wearing. He had a gold-coloured tie clip, glasses, and it seems little else. "His behaviour is rather pitiful as he is looking around slowly ... Patient makes a pleasant appearance in his way of not overemphasising his presence here," read his clinical notes from a few days after he is picked up. There is a trace of compassion: "Patient appears rather insecure and somehow bewildered in his own well-worn and shabby clothing." English Textiles, fallen on hard times. "Patient displayed paranoid tendencies and wondered why I did not make enquiries into his past and his business. He assumed that I wanted to overlook this failure in his past."

This failure in his past. "Can't you give me another chance?" he had asked my mother.

Among his belongings is also listed "1 Jewish cap". I never knew him to own a yarmulke, a kippah, never saw him wear one except the time when he read from the Torah at Jerry's bar mitzvah.

Despite the "Jewish cap", the conference report of the Ontario Department of Health, Mental Health Branch, in June 1967 describes him as "57 years of age; Roman Catholic; Merchant; Married." It is noted that he was in the Polish underground during the war. But it soon becomes clear that my father never tells his doctors the full extent of what he survived. Clinical summary, June 1967: "He stated he was always very close to his family, but he recalls many hardships and heartbreaking experiences during the war years. His mother, two sisters and three brothers were accidentally killed during the war."

Accidentally. There was not yet a common language for Holocaust survivors to talk about what had happened to them. There was shame and humiliation. The word Holocaust, and the particularity of the Jewish genocide, was only just coming into use, due in part to the Eichmann trial in 1961.

In 1946 a Russian-born American psychology professor, David Boder, went to Europe to interview, mostly with anthropological detachment, survivors. Largely ignored for fifty years, his recordings began to attract attention after they were transferred to tape by the Library of Congress in 1995.

When an interviewee mentions Auschwitz, Boder doesn't know what or where that is. When a survivor, Nellie, talks about stragglers being shot during the march from Auschwitz to Birkenau, Boder says, "What, were they shooting them like sentenced people, putting them to the wall?" Oh no, Nellie says. "All the route was bordered with corpses, you see."

Boder didn't see. He had no notion of the soldiers of a civilised country picking off prisoners for convenience, for sport. The survivors were returning from another dimension. Even twenty years later, no one seemed to think the experiences of a Jewish man who went through the war in Poland and somehow lost his entire family might inform his current pathology.

Sometimes in the records my father is Jewish. "Mr Wichtel is of Hebrew faith," writes Miss Crawford, his social worker, in May 1968. She is sending a letter on his behalf to a Mr Bronstein of the Hebrew Benevolent Society. There seems to be an avoidance of the word "Jew". Perhaps my father was by then frightened of being seen as Jewish. I've wondered about the two spellings of his name in the file. Maybe he encouraged the "Witchell" version when presenting himself as a Catholic. Perhaps, having landed up in a place with few Jews, he could get more help from the local Catholic Church. On the run, Uncle Paul grew his "Polish moustache".

Miss Crawford sounds kind. She spells his name correctly. When she writes to Mr Bronstein she notes: "He is without friends, family and financial resources." She talks him up: "He has been a person of good ability, speaks several languages … but is somewhat lost in our setting." In that entire huge file my father is most recognisably himself when Miss Crawford writes about him. I search to see if she is still alive but can find no trace of her.

She notes he has a wife and children. "We believe them to be in New Zealand ... Mr Wichtel has been very independent and is hurt and confused by the rejection of both his wife and his brother." She asks Mr Bronstein for a small grant of money.

My father sometimes offers alternative versions of reality. After his bankruptcy, according to the history in his hospital notes, his family moved to Toronto. In fact, we were gone: he went alone. "After he went bankrupt, and later was unable to work, his wealthy brother offered his home to the patient's family. Mrs Witchell continues to live with these relatives in New Jersey. ... The brother is ... putting the two girls through university." This would account for the letters we got when I was fourteen, sent via Sy and Mollie. He seemed to think we were in New Jersey living the high life, not shipwrecked on Milford Beach. Later in his clinical notes I read: "He spoke of an impending divorce though at one time he stated that his wife and children were in New Zealand. His memory is somewhat blunted and in mood he is depressed."

Those caring for him have simply taken down what my father said. His wife and children are being taken care of by his rich brother. We girls will be put through university. His family is gone and his brother's wife is to blame: "The patient reports that he couldn't get on with his sister-in-law and left the home." He was constantly reminded by his sister-in-law, he tells the doctors, "that his brother had become 'a business tycoon' and he was a failure." He believes she has people watching him and reporting to her. "He thinks that information has reached the hospital as to his character and that he has been disgraced by it. He also feels this information has been withheld from him."

It's as if the horror he has kept at bay by building a family, working at his store, playing his balalaika, has finally overwhelmed him. When the Nazis set out to destroy the Jews of Europe, one of the first things they did was take away their means of making a living. Financial ruin has tipped my father back into that abyss. "Patient was always independent, and his pride is hurt that he cannot support his family but has to depend on his brother to do it." Maybe it's best to think his brother is caring for us. That way he is still providing for us. "I will do my best for you, you can be sure," he had written to us.

THE NARRATIVES WE CONSTRUCT TO GET BY: until the arrival of the file, I could believe the version in which he had become insane, beyond all reach, nothing we could have done. End of story. But then everything I thought I knew turned out to be wrong.

In these elliptical accounts some answers can be found. Sy, despite his own collapsing business and marriage, had continued for a time to help my father. Miss Crawford writes asking him for money. My mother in later life told me she destroyed the correspondence she had with Brockville. She couldn't bear to keep it. The letter from Miss Crawford to Uncle Sy makes you see why she might burn such letters, so as to never have to read them again: "He is very lonely," Miss Crawford writes. "Have you any news of his wife and children? We wondered, too, if once again you could send him a little pocket money, so he could go to the canteen, or on a little outing during the summer months."

Information about his life before he met my mother is minimal, just the names of his father and mother. The names of his children are not recorded. There is a document from the newly formed Department of Manpower and Immigration confirming he is a Canadian citizen. The medical conference when he is admitted to Brockville has concluded he is suffering from Parkinson's disease, and psychosis caused by cerebral arteriosclerosis—hardening of the arteries of the brain.

On July 19, 1967 there are signs of optimism. "He states that he feels a lot better since treatment was started... He can now use a spoon and fork very steadily... He proudly shows how he can do this."

October 27, 1967: "He confessed today he was a little frightened (he anticipated that we would be giving him E.C.T.) but he denies being depressed and indeed he was quite cheerful at interview." Attempts are being made to place him back into the community. That month he is moved to Ward G, a more open part of the hospital. A letter is sent to Sy seeking permission for him to have a bunion operation so he can wear his sandals.

By February 1968 an exasperated note is creeping into the medical conference reports. "He is now constantly insisting that he leave the hospital to resume his occupation. However, his physical condition is deteriorating and he is quite delusional." As a compromise, Miss Crawford attempts to organise a place for him in a Jewish home in Toronto, or to get financial assistance for him to live in the community there.

In April 1968, a wrenching detail: "May go to Wizard of Oz downtown." An internet search confirms there was a production by the Brockville Operatic Society that month. The movie *The Wizard of Oz* screened on television every Easter when I was a child. Our family would watch it together: Judy Garland clicking the heels of her ruby slippers, chanting, "There's no place like home."

As plans advance for my father to try independent life back in Toronto, he grows anxious. "He had mixed feelings of wanting to leave hospital and of being very afraid of the future alone in the community," Miss Crawford writes on May 8. The plan is eventually abandoned. "Since then, Mr Wichtel has been very quiet going about his business around the hospital."

It's all downhill in 1969. He is prescribed Valium (tranquilliser), Artane (tremors), Peritrate (angina), Maalox (acid stomach), Paraldehyde (sedative for sleep), and Tarasan (anti-psychotic). In March Sy is sent a letter: "We are pleased to advise you that your brother Benjamin Witchell was admitted to Lapalme Nursing Home in Embrun Ontario on March 12 under the Homes for Special Care Programme." It is hoped the nursing home will be a better environment for him. "Rate Paid to Home $8.50 per day. Estimated cost of comforts and clothes per year $120.00. Pin Money on Hand: Nil."

Things don't go well in Embrun. He accuses the nurses and doctor of giving him "needles" to dope him, and contacts first a lawyer and then the police. "Patient called the police on three successive days from Casselman, Rockland and Long Sault, requesting they investigate immediately."

Does that mean he actually went to these three towns? Casselman is seventeen minutes by car from Embrun, Rockland thirty-seven minutes and Long Sault forty-four minutes. During the war he didn't take powerlessness without putting up a fight. He isn't giving up this time either, but the strategies that served him then—running, resisting, trusting no one—are not working so well. "Patient became a public nuisance," reads the report from Lapalme. And there is the handwritten note to the Psych: "This man simply cannot stay here."

While my father is in the Lapalme Nursing Home my mother is trying to initiate divorce proceedings. I read in the Brockville file: "this hospital could not give further information regarding the above-named patient's condition without the written consent of the next of kin." She should contact the patient's doctor at Lapalme Nursing Home, and also his legal guardian, the Public Trustee. It is a shock to realise that my mother, still my father's wife, must go through the Public Trustee to get information about him.

When she tells us in the tiny living room of the house in Williamson Avenue that our father is in a psychiatric hospital in Canada, I am eighteen, living with my boyfriend. Why don't I say, "What is this place?" Why don't I write? When my mother goes to Japan, Philip and I have no parents to speak of, no place to call home: this is all I have to offer in my defence.

"Indigent" is how my father is described at the nursing home. He lacks the resources for even a little outing in the summer months. He is sent back to Brockville on June 22, 1969. "Condition of hair: grey, abundant. No apparent vermin." He needs a haircut.

The home has sent a patient evaluation. "Behaviour: reserved. Demands attention: often. Complaining: often. Responses: sociable." He is apparently fastidious in his personal habits. He has "strong prejudices about persons or things". His smoking is "moderate", his sexual interest "seldom". He enjoys writing and TV. I wonder what he wrote and what became of it. Did he write to us? I worry there were letters we never received.

Back in Brockville he is assessed. June 25, 1969: "He worries about his future and presents paranoid ideas concerning his personal and family history." July 3: "Psychological testing was attempted without success," Dr G notes wearily. "Mr Witchell is a person of good appearance and manners and the impression given was that he is of at least average intelligence. He appeared very confused and unhappy with the way he has been shifted between institutions and is under the impression that certain of his relatives are after his money."

There are other complaints. "He claims he is awakened every night and given 'needles' and that there is 'a little engine' used by the doctors to keep him awake nights. A check with the ward staff revealed this to be totally delusional." It's touching that Dr G has checked as to the existence of the "little engine".

On September 8 there is a letter addressed to Dr B, the staff psychiatrist, signed by my father in a shaky hand. My niece Nicola has pointed out that the body of the letter is in a different handwriting; perhaps it was written with the help of the indefatigable Miss Crawford.

"I am taking the liberty to explain why I had the occasion to go to a lawyer in Brockville. After many futile attempts to explain my situation to several doctors I have no relatives who can help me, I felt I was left with no other choice than to seek the advice of a lawyer. Under no circumstances did I chastise or defame any of the hospital's doctors. ... for two years since I have been here I have had full privileges and have never abused them this being the first time I have lost my privileges. I realise now I made a mistake seeking a lawyer's advice without permission, but I did so with no bad intentions and would like to apologise for it. I would appreciate it then very much, Dr B, if you would re-initiate my privileges, or at least give me some start on them again, so I could regain your trust."

By then his clinical records show that my father, even within the rhythms and routines of the Psych, continues to be a displaced person. "He does not participate in recreational activities and does not work. He has no occupational therapy and no physical therapy. He has ground privileges but does not visit home." Despite his attempts to explain his situation, they don't seem to realise he has no home.

In his letter to Dr B he sounds reasonable, polite, desperate. He must have written again in November, although that letter is not in the file, just the blandly professional reply: "Dear Mr Wichtel, Thank you for your letter of 27th of November. I think that you should discuss your problem with your doctor." But my father has tried that a month earlier: "Dear Sir, I am desirous of having an appointment with you at your convenience. There are some matters which I would prefer to discuss with you."

Letters, lawyers, nothing helps. On November 26 my father is "very hostile and argumentative. He is suspicious and has the feeling everyone is mistreating him. Patient accuses ward personnel of giving him injections when he is fast asleep. He claims that someone burnt his clothes, which is not a fact."

The following year, 1970, sounds like a war zone. My father "requires some supervision and is irritable at times. He shows mental deterioration. He does not work; no recreation. Hit on side of face by patient X."

In September he is struck again, resulting in "a cut of approximately 1¼ inches on left cheek. X-ray examination recommended—negative. Notification not necessary. He has no visitors. No further action necessary."

Clinical record, September 2, 1970. "Attendants' notes state when he goes downtown very often he is looking for lawyers and complaining about mistreatment and persecution."

In October 1970 he is offered L-Dopa, a new medication for Parkinson's. The neurologist Oliver Sacks will write in his 1973 book *Awakenings* of the dramatic if short-lived effects of L-Dopa being administered in 1969 to patients who have been immobilised for decades in a sort of trance state by "sleeping sickness"—encephalitis lethargica.

On October 6 my father is "very uncooperative and refusing to undergo all these examinations, stating that he is not an experimental animal for the use of some new drugs on him. It was, and still at present, is impossible to explain or persuade him."

He knows what sort of experiments can take place on people who have been deprived of their freedom. "He is obviously very delusional and paranoidal all the time in his thinking, is very unsatisfied with everything on the ward."

The doctors can't reach him. He is in the stream of history.

November 6: "He is very disabled and largely confined to a wheelchair."

Later that month he is persuaded to start L-Dopa. Dr K notes he is "less hysterical and manipulating, occasionally he forgets about his 'shakes' too. Sharp-witted, clever, attention-seeking, becoming immediately the 'lame bird' when he finds the proper audience." My father is back in the forest, trying every trick he knows to survive.

There are concerns relating to the new drug regime: "As a possible side effect … he is sweating profusely and we expect that he will lose some weight."

From about November 22, there are further symptoms, including "a rapid reaction after the morning medication … He became flushed, his pulse was running and he showed no temperature elevation."

His doctor continues to attribute these symptoms to a reaction to medication. "Last night this man suddenly developed fever with no sign of cough or congestion practically and we put him under an antibiotic umbrella. Today he lapsed into a coma in the early morning hours and his condition is very precarious."

It seems he also fell. An accident and injury report dated November 25 states he has a large bruise on the right side of his face. "Time and cause of injury unknown."

His bedside nursing notes for November 26 chart a vertiginous decline. 12.00: "Appetite good." 0800: Juice, 7oz, accepted very slowly." 0900: "Does not respond." 12.30: "Breathing laboured and shallow." 13.00: "Pronounced dead per Dr K. Body and clothing sent to morgue." His only visitor was a priest. He gave him the last rites of a church of which he was not a member, in the name of a God he didn't believe in. He was sixty years old.

Because of the fall and the bruising, an autopsy is ordered. Cause of death: "Acute bilateral broncho-pneumonia, 3–5 days. Contributing cause: psychosis with cerebral atherosclerosis. Parkinsonism." The consultant who prescribed the new medication will later report: "The flush and sweats which he developed following his L-Dopa were due, I think, to his developing pneumonia and not side-effect from his medication." The report does not speculate on whether the outcome would have been different had his pneumonia been diagnosed earlier.

From the Report of Institutional Burial, Department of Health for Ontario, Mental Hospitals Division: "The remains were buried in a suitably prepared grave and Father Farrell officiated. Relatives and friends present: None." To read this is to feel like an accessory to a crime.

THE FILE HAS MUCH DETAIL of the kind that is full of devils. In the final summary of my father's case, the Brockville doctor wrote: "During his hospitalization he showed a great amount of manipulation, hysterical behavior and was prone to babble silly ideas whenever he was able to catch a listener. When his plannings were upset or unsuccessful he was soon running into an hysterical, expansive state with paranoid colouring."

In 2013 I get the chance to interview an American-born, London-based psychiatrist, Stephen Grosz, for the *Listener*. Grosz, whose father was also a Holocaust survivor, has written a lovely little book *The Examined Life*, in which he presents case studies of some of his patients. It is full of small perspective-altering epiphanies. Paranoia, Grosz notes, has its uses. He gives the example of a successful woman who, whenever she came home from a business trip, was plagued by fears that her door had been wired to blow up when she turned the key. It emerged that she hated coming back to a cold empty flat. It was better to feel targeted by nameless enemies out to destroy her than to feel no one was thinking of her. "Her paranoia," Grosz writes, "shielded her from the catastrophe of indifference." Maybe my father's feeling that someone was always watching, always plotting against him, was better than feeling abandoned, forgotten.

The doctors noted impatiently that he was psychotic, paranoid, delusional, a public nuisance. Actually, his actions made perfect sense. Dreadful things had been done to him, twice. The Nazis and their collaborators had taken away his family and murdered them in cold blood: his mother Rozalia, his sisters and brothers, their children. Then, despite his best efforts to carry on, he lost everything again—his wife and children, his business, his freedom. He sought help from a lawyer, from the polizei. He still believed in a future where he could get some justice. Once again no one listened. The help never came.

CHAPTER 16

The Psych

Wanted To Come To New Zealand.

Jewish Immigrant Aid Services, Montreal, 1965

BROCKVILLE. WHY ON EARTH, the man at the ticket desk in the Montreal train station wants to know, do we want to go to Brockville? Long story, we say. We don't tell it. Where to begin when each fact of the matter begs a metastasising mass of questions to which there are no reasonable answers? You could spend a lifetime trying to make sense of it.

I could have said my father was a Polish Jew who was in the Warsaw Ghetto and jumped from a train bound for Treblinka. I could have tried to explain that he was lost, twice. That everything he had was taken from him, twice. That he, a Jew, a survivor, a broken fighter at the extreme edge of human experience, ended up in a Catholic cemetery with nothing on the stone but a misspelt name, and dates that spanned an abyss, 1910–1970, with nothing of his true identity left. I could have given the sort of reply that makes a person wish they had never asked.

I could have said, "My father has been lost and we are going to find him" but then I would have cried in the Montreal train station. We say we're looking for a family grave. The man shakes his head— Brockville!—and hands over the tickets.

It's June 2015. We'd been planning to go back to Poland. More research, more dark tourism, more vodka. The idea was to set up in Warsaw for at least a week. Chris would seek out more monuments to murder and memorial, and we would continue our tour of the death camps of Eastern Europe. It's our idea of a good time.

Then my father's file arrived. For days after reading it I catch myself trudging along, staring at the ground. Grief, I find, has a metallic taste, like blood in the mouth.

There are phone calls to make to Brockville at dawn to account for the time difference. I am not sleeping anyway. The Ontario Ministry of Health, the undertakers, the cemetery—the bleak roll call of a lonely death. I start with the manager of Oakland Cemetery. His name is Dale Trickey. This time I am on solid ground. I have dates. I have documentation.

"I'm calling from New Zealand," I announce confidently. "My father was buried at your cemetery on November 30, 1970."

"I'll check my book," Dale says. No, he says, when he comes back. No Benjamin Wichtel.

"How about Benjamin Witchell?"

No. "You must have the wrong year."

"It can't be wrong. I'm sitting here staring at the Brockville Psychiatric Hospital Statement of Death and the Report of Institutional Burial."

"Hmm," Dale says, "was he Catholic by any chance?"

"Well no," I sigh. "But since you ask…" Cue the long story of a Polish Jewish Holocaust survivor who ends up claiming to be a non-practising Catholic for reasons that must have made sense at the time.

"Try Brockville's St Francis Xavier Catholic Church," Dale says. They have a section at the cemetery.

No, no Ben Wichtel or Witchell there either, says the woman at the St Francis Xavier office. The late Father Farrell officiated, I say. She knows of him, but again there's no record. My father liked to fly under the radar, but even given the increasingly Kafkaesque convolutions of this search things are becoming farcical. Short of posthumous abduction by grave-robbing aliens, my father has to be there.

"Leave it with me," Dale Trickey says. "Call me in a couple of days."

There's an email from Dale waiting next day at dawn. "Dear Diane, I found your dad's grave in St Francis Cemetery, lot 26 section I. There is a small marker. Talk later."

Lot 26, section one. After nearly half a century he is found. There's joy, exhilaration, trepidation. What have I done? I fear the effect on my relationship with my sister, which has become increasingly fragile due to our different experiences of our family's past. I fear the effect on everyone. The past now has a grave and a marker. His name is misspelled, no one at the hospital bothered to apply for an official death certificate, and the cemetery failed to record his burial, but there he is. I feel irrationally fond of Dale Trickey.

"We're going to Brockville," Chris says.

In the meantime I continue phoning every place in Brockville that might have a connection. I find out that the hospital where he died, the place the locals called the Psych, is now abandoned. There's still a forensic unit for criminals on the campus. We can visit the grounds and look around but we can't enter the old buildings.

Lapalme Nursing Home in Embrun, just over an hour's drive from Brockville, where my father was sent for three torrid months, is long demolished. Someone suggests I ring the Township of Russell Public Library and check for records. The wonderfully helpful librarian—"We don't get many calls from New Zealand"—says all the home's archives have been destroyed but she knows the daughter of the family who used to run it. She emails back to say the daughter recalls my father's name and will ask her mother and a retired nurse who worked there if they have any information. Then things go very quiet.

Eventually the woman reports that my father was there for only a brief time and no one can remember much. I write pleading emails. I know he was a difficult client but even if there is nothing good to say I would love to have a chance to speak to anyone who was there at the time. No dice. Either they can't remember him or would rather not. The librarian sends a photo from the 1960s of the brick building that is no longer there. We add a stop at Embrun to our improbable itinerary.

So our three weeks away will now begin with a week in Canada, followed by five days in Poland, with a day in Berlin on the way. Seeing we're now going to be in North America we add a visit to New York and New Jersey to talk about developments with Jerry and Linda. Joe is not well, so no visit to Allentown this time. We'll phone him from Manhattan.

Then it will be on to London and a Wolfson College anniversary at Cambridge. We could have delayed, planned a less hectic trip, but after waiting so long I cannot wait a moment longer. On hearing our crammed itinerary my six-year-old grandson Sam gives me a hard look. "If you are going to five countries, Di-nana, you should go for five weeks." Even he thinks we're mad.

Dale Trickey assures me the grave is there but it's impossible to shake the feeling that it will turn out to be some sort of mistake. We first fly into Vancouver, with three days to look around the old family places. Being there sends me into the spiral of psychic dissonance that happens when past and present, kept carefully separate for so long, clash. Chris and I argue our way around the city.

Nicola is with us briefly. Like her father she's a wonderful travel companion and a calming influence. She's heading home to Prince Edward Island for a holiday from her veterinary course at Massey University and has a few hours before catching a plane to Toronto.

We stay in a hotel in which the décor seems not to have changed since I lived in Vancouver. There is, ominously, a giant plunger in the bathroom, but the breakfast of bagels and cream cheese is good and it's a short walk to Pender Street. The shop that housed English Textiles, and the tenements at the back that housed immigrants and refugees, are all gone. Hudson's Bay and Army & Navy, the department stores my harried mother would herd us into, having to strip off boots, leggings, ear muffs and mittens in winter and wrestle us back into them when we left, are still in business. Chinatown, too, remains, and so does Modernize Tailors, which has been in Pender Street since 1913. It's closed or I would have run in and said, "Does anyone here remember my father?" Although it's now certain that he is lying dead in Brockville, I can't shake the feeling I will find him in Pender Street.

We head to dinner in the gentrified Gastown district, a block away. The sight of so many people begging, many of them disabled, is a shock. Vancouver has changed. A woman identifies us as tourists and says, "You don't want to go down there. It isn't safe." At dinner a man who cannot lift up his head comes over to ask for money. "Go away, John," the waiter says. The amount of food we have in front of us is obscene. Nicola asks the restaurant to pack up a box and takes it over to John.

Next day Chris and I set off in search of the old family homes. First we go to the North Shore by bus over the Lionsgate Bridge, then trek up familiar streets to 4414 Canterbury Crescent, the last house we owned, where my father yelled at my mother for refusing to ask Sy for help and for agreeing to ask Sy for help, where they came and took away the piano.

A neighbour comes out on the porch.

"Can I help you?" He sounds a little suspicious.

"I used to live here," I say vaguely. It feels as though either the man is a ghost or I am.

Chris is digging me in the ribs. "Tell him your name," he hisses.

"We were the Wichtel family," I say.

"Oh, sure," the man says. "I remember the Wichtels."

The past is roaring in my ears. If I squint hard I can remember this man, Sandy Thomson—tall, lanky, normal, with an overbite—coming across the lawn to see what's up when my father is standing in our front yard shouting about a septic-tank pipe that one of the neighbourhood kids has thrown a rock at and broken.

Sandy remembers the episode. It wasn't one of his kids.

We stand talking on the doorstep until we are invited in. Now in their eighties, Sandy and his wife Margo were much younger than my parents. Margo, who is getting ready to go off to tennis, is wearing a housecoat like my mother used to wear in the morning. I feel a wash of grief for my parents, who lived there, just over the fence, before their lives fell apart.

Sandy and Margo tell us about the neighbours, the kids with whom we would play games of *Monopoly* that went on for days. There were the Shugs, and the family who lived next door on the other side. I babysat their two children when I was twelve. Louise, aged four, used to wake with night terrors, her unseeing eyes wide open. I had to get medicine into her and wait until she stopped screaming. The father, it was whispered, suffered from depression.

Up the road was Keith Milton. He was cute and nice and had a sunny rec room and a portable device you could pop a 45 record into. I am happy to hear he ended up playing in a band.

The Beveridges lived down the road. I played Barbies with Sheila, who had a little brother called Jimmy. Once I went to a party there and the whole family played *Dictionary*. We never did things like that.

Across the road is a modern house in the place of the one where the Gardners used to live. Carol Gardner was my sister's friend and had a little brother called Jimmy. Everyone had a little brother called Jimmy. The children went to a Catholic school. Once when I was visiting them I was shocked to hear her mother say Carol had got her period.

Margo describes my mother as "very nice" and remembers her making a delicious dessert with cream and apricots. Once, at our house, she'd seen her serve my father hors d'oeuvres in a little crystal dish on a stool by his armchair. When he knocked it over and broke the dish my mother was annoyed. I wonder if my father was already getting shaky.

There's a slight look of panic when I ask about him. "Oh, we didn't really see much of him. He worked a lot," Margo says.

At one point I blurt out, "Did you think we were weird?"

Oh no, they say.

We go outside and I peer over the fence into our old backyard. There's the room I shared with Ros. In winter, if we were lucky, we would wake to see the window lit with the spectral glow that meant it had snowed in the night. I almost expect to see Dukey trying to bury her toast and honey in the hard earth. The house looks exhausted. We got there just in time, Sandy says. It's going to be demolished. Prices have gone sky-high in the neighbourhood—1.3 million dollars for that place across the road, imagine. Where the Wichtels once lived something more substantial will be built.

Sandy insists on getting out the car and driving us around the neighbourhood. We go down Highland Boulevard and look at our last house. It's opposite Capilano Heights Elementary, where my little brother Jeff could have gone, where Uldis put in the lawn, and where my father would appear in the doorway looking lost; where he said to my mother, "Can't you give me another chance?"

We go through Edgemont Village where we kids would go for comics, and where there were excursions to the deli for matzo and hot smoked salmon. We drive by my old school, Handsworth High, closed for the summer. I still remember the school song: "Hail to thee our alma mater / Loyal and true every son and daughter." We would sing a subversive version: "Hail to Handsworth Jail / Hail to thee our penitentiary."

I want to walk down what we called "the cut", a steep ravine that was a shortcut home. Boys would make giant snowballs and drop them on us as we ran the gauntlet. You could slide down to the bottom on your school bag and part-way up the other side when the creek was frozen. But Sandy is waiting to drop us at Capilano Canyon, with its giant suspension bridge. Dad used to take us there and rock the bridge to frighten us when we crossed. Amid the old-growth firs and walkways in the treetops that weren't there in our day, I get mixed up about where I'm supposed to meet Chris and we have an argument. The past is exhausting.

Next day we go to Kerrisdale to see the house I still dream of, with its gabled bedrooms and secret door to the attic inside a wardrobe, the house where you could hide out in the basement avoiding school, and where Dad brought home the girlie movie. On the way we stop at the elementary school, which looks largely unchanged except that the beautiful dogwood tree in the playground is gone, and take the familiar walk home to 3389 West 43rd. Emboldened by our encounter with Sandy and Margo I consider knocking on the door, but something makes me hold back. My enchanted house looks like it's fallen under an evil spell. Shrubs have grown up high, right in front of the windows. Little light must get in and it would be impossible to see out.

I cross the road and knock on the door of what used to be the Mitchells' house. There were five children—Barbara, Pat, Billy, Bofer and baby Sam. Mr Mitchell was seldom home. Mrs Mitchell played the piano and taught us songs from *South Pacific*. I felt comfortable there.

A woman answers the door. She's pleasant but doesn't invite us in. She is too young to recall the Wichtels, or Doreen and Warren who lived in the house next door to hers. She says an Asian family have been living in our house. She believes the elderly woman has recently died. In Kerrisdale the past is another country where there's no one home.

IN MONTREAL WE MEET UP with Nicola again, and my brother Jeff, and visit the address on the last letter we have from my father: 1624 Sherbrook Street West. It's a brick building that used to be a boarding house. What was Dad doing while he lived in this place? We know from his file that when he was picked up by the police in Cornwall, confused and frightened, trying to cross the border into the US, he had in his belongings a "Jewish cap". This suggests he was in touch with the Jewish community here. Maybe he still had contacts from when he arrived in Canada in 1947 and lived in the city for a few months.

IN JANUARY 2016, four months before we set off on this trip, another bombshell had landed in my inbox. I had got in touch with another wonderful Canadian, Alan Greenberg of the Jewish Genealogical Society, a volunteer organisation helping people like me do searches like ours. He was intrigued by this request from the ends of the earth. There was no Ben Wichtel or Witchell in the society's archives, but after reading my recounting of the story—"Your whole saga sounds so painful"—he had offered to get in touch with Montreal's Jewish Immigrant Aid Society to see if my father had had any contact with it during his time in Montreal in 1965.

"We have a hit with JIAS records!" Alan wrote. He'd attached a copy of a hand-written index card dated November 26, 1965. There was little information, just my father's name, correctly spelled, his address in Montreal, and his city of birth, Warsaw. Then I noticed six words neatly printed at the bottom of the card: "Wants to go to New Zealand."

I sat staring at the words, stunned. All this time I had wondered if my father had never really tried to come, if the story that he was to follow us was a fiction to cover up a final separation. After we arrived in New Zealand I felt he'd abandoned us. Now here was hard evidence that just over a year after we left he was trying to join us.

Alan advised me to contact Janice Rosen at the society for the rest of the file. Soon she sent it by email. It revealed that my father sought help with the paperwork required to travel to New Zealand. It contained the phone number of the New Zealand Trade Commission and a short history of tribulation: "Wife Patricia née Scantlebury, 2 girls and boy live in New Zealand since one year. Lost business and house in Vancouver (Haberdashery and Clo.)."Then the words, again, that can't be read without tears: "Wants to go to New Zealand and join family."

The society had informed him that all he needed to proceed was his Canadian passport. The file contained his passport number; this will help me to finally, after failed applications under Canada's Access to Information Act, get his Canadian immigration and citizenship file. With the information about his application for citizenship in 1954, there's a passport photograph from 1965. Taken from microfiche, it's a negative. Chris manages to invert it and suddenly there he is. It's the only photo we have from his later years, possibly the last ever taken that was not for police files. He is smartly suited, his tie neatly knotted. His hair looks dark and well groomed. He looks older, wan, but there's a small hopeful smile for the camera. When he was living in the house at 1624 Sherbrook Street West, Montreal, he was trying to come to New Zealand. He didn't abandon us; we abandoned him.

FROM MONTREAL IT'S A SHORT, tense, two-and-a-half-hour drive to Brockville. We stop off at Embrun. Perhaps it was the boredom here that helped drive my father mad. Where Lapalme Nursing Home once stood there's nothing to see but a forlorn statue of the Virgin

Mary presiding over a vacant lot with a view to a water tower. There is now a smaller rest home next door. They've been having some sort of gathering and we speak to a man who is coming out. He takes us in and we talk to the woman running the home. Her mother once worked at Lapalme but is very old and unlikely to know anything about my father.

We have lunch in the sort of place you find off the beaten track in eastern Canada: a Mom and Pop eatery that reminds you of your grandmother's parlour but with a more extensive menu. I'm not really hungry. We dally. I'm afraid to get to Brockville.

Finally, Oakland Cemetery, 1524 County Road, Brockville. It's a dazzling Ontario summer's day. The cemetery is more serene and cared for than I imagined it would be. There are trees. There are birds. We find the St Francis Xavier section. Markers of graves of inmates from the psychiatric hospital are set into the lawn, each with a stark inscription: name, year of birth, year of death.

We can't find my father. I knew it. There's a panicked call to Dale Trickey. In a minute or two he pulls up in a shiny red ute. "You were so close," he says. There it is, on the end of a row, by the path. Dale has cleared away the grass from a grave never visited in forty-five years. Family and friends present at the burial: none. We stand and look, take photographs, kneel down to make contact. We place stones and sea glass brought from New Zealand, tucking them in around the stone so the lawnmower won't scatter them. "Hey, Grandpa," says Nicola. She has her father's easy way with people, living or dead. I whisper useless words: Dad. I love you. I'm sorry.

Next stop: the Psych. It's not far away. Around the side, fenced off, is the bleak-looking forensic unit that houses, among others, Russell Johnson, a sexual sadist, murderer and nechrophiliac who scaled apartment buildings up to fifteen storeys to kill seven women between 1973 and 1977. Russell Johnson is your worst nightmare.

Ben Wichtel's grave in St Francis Xavier Cemetery, Brockville, Ontario, in 2015.

There are old greenhouses. We stop by what were once stables for horses and cows. The place had its own farm until 1967, the year my father arrived, and continued to have gardens growing produce. We stop to talk to a caretaker. He tells us the inmates of the forensic unit are sometimes allowed out to help out around the place. "They can lift logs I couldn't pick up. They don't know their own strength," he muses. "They're just like normal people but you don't turn your back on them."

The old buildings where my father was housed are abandoned. Through the windows are corridors and rooms that appear untouched since the last patients left. At the front, verandahs look out over the lawns. Nicola likes to imagine her grandfather sat there and found some comfort in the gardens, the squirrels, the birds. The sign for his wards—Ward K, Ward G—remain. "Visiting Hours 11am–8pm.

Please sign in and wear visitor badge." A security guard drives up to enquire what we think we are doing. One of our family used to live here, we say. "That's okay," he says. "It's just we've had trouble with people breaking in." It probably used to be the other way around.

Brockville turns out to be quite a pretty town where everything is a tribute to Sir Isaac Brock, who defended what was then the province of Upper Canada against the United States. A statue by the St Lawrence River depicts another more recent Brockville identity, an eccentric sheltering beneath a holey umbrella while pushing a pram with a bird in it. It seems okay to be a bit unhinged here. After dinner we say goodbye to Jeff and Nicola. In the morning Chris and I will take the train to Toronto, my father's last city of residence before the Psych, and then fly to New York.

I understand now something I found bizarre and primitive when I read Mary Gordon's book *The Shadow Man*, about her lost Jewish father. She had said she wanted to hold his bones. In the end she dug them up and had them reburied where she thought her father should be. We must disinter my father and take him, finally, to New Zealand, I have decided. Jeff and Chris, demonstrating the need to have good people around to tell you when you are heading dangerously off piste, suggest a less insane plan: we will make a new headstone. It will have the history no one at Brockville asked him about. It will correctly spell his name. It will say who he was and what he managed to do in a world out to get him, a world gone mad.

CHAPTER 17

Comparing notes

Never forget you are a Wichtel.

Uncle Sy, summer 1971

BEFORE WE SET OFF for that first drive to Brockville in 2015, Jeff and I had sat down in an Airbnb apartment in downtown Montreal. We've never really talked about Dad, my brother and I, not more than fragments. Jeff was only five the last time he saw his father.

"I can remember going to his tailor shop," he says. "I have quite vivid memories of that for some reason: very dark and lots of strange equipment, things for pressing clothes. And I have a vision of an old porcelain sink in the back, with copper staining in it.

"My memories are of him coming home with a chocolate bar, or something to spoil me. I remember him buying me a little pedal car—that was a big day in my life." Jeff would have been two at the time. Dad also bought him a toy rifle. It was this he shouldered in the backyard at Kerrisdale, and, looking down the sight, said, "I once saw a woman have her breasts shot off."

Jeff remembers just once being the focus of one of our father's sudden rages. "It was at the dinner table. I wouldn't eat my peas. He lost his temper, flew off the handle. Peas ended up flying all over the kitchen." As soon as he conjures up this scene I'm convinced I remember it too.

"I suspect I was protected a lot from what was going down in the latter years," he says. He spent most of his time with Mum. "I don't understand why I didn't go to kindergarten. I was probably more than ready for it. Maybe she just wanted the company."

When he escaped the house there were adventures. One time he and a friend took off with their toy guns, headed in the direction of Grouse Mountain as the crow flies, climbing over people's fences. My mother was about to call the police when they finally returned.

"I can remember going to Capilano Canyon," Jeff says. "It was one of the rare times when Dad and I did something together. He liked to scare me about the bears, which I took quite seriously. I'm not sure I looked at him as a father figure. He was almost like a benign uncle."

He recalls no sadness when we left. "I remember backing out of the driveway and waving goodbye to my friend Bradley out the car window. I was probably told Dad was going to follow, that this was just a temporary arrangement. My life was so focused on Mum that if she'd said to jump off a cliff I would have."

In New Zealand, with our mother working, Jeff's life as the longed-for boy, the little prince, was gone. "I came home from school early one day and panicked because no one was home. That's how I got this scar," he says, indicating his hand. "I broke the window trying to get into Nana's house.

"Once I left my bike at someone's place. Grandpa got mad and strung the bike up in the garage for a couple of weeks to teach me a lesson. I don't think I'd ever been disciplined in my life before."

I don't remember in those early years in exile discussing our changed circumstances with Ros or Jeff. Mum being with us provided a measure of security—she and I were close, always—and Jeff says it was that way for him too. "We were in survival mode," he says. "I knew it was tough. If I lost my shoes it was a major issue because Mum had to buy more and we didn't have the money. I never questioned the situation; I'm embarrassed to say that. For some reason I forgot about my father."

Well, we had been teleported to another dimension. "We might have been on Mars," Jeff agrees. "We were just trying to fit in. In those days immigrants on the North Shore were quite unusual." Not to mention a solo mother. "We were a very odd family. We either played in the vacant lots or down at the beach. It was a childhood I'm kind of nostalgic about."

Then Jeff went with Mum and Stew to Japan. "Even I could see Mum was under terrible stress," he says. "She was a wreck for a whole variety of reasons, physical and mental. Soon after we got to Japan I was told Dad had died. By then another five years had elapsed without him in my life. And I had Stew." With Jeff, Stew had perhaps the least complicated relationship in his life. They loved each other.

Jeff survived the sometimes wild expat life in Japan, where Mum and Stew partied hard at the Officers' Club. "I look back and see it probably wasn't the best example of parenting and we were lucky to come through it unscathed." When he was older Mum talked to him about it. "Up until that point she never let me know how desperate she had been—other than her anxiousness over money: I picked that up pretty quickly. We had nothing."

When our mother was dying her younger sisters asked her if they could send along the hospital chaplain. "Oh, all right," she said. She didn't like to say no. When her sisters had gone and the chaplain turned up, she whispered to me to send her away: "I can say my own Hail Marys." Whoever God was, she would face him on her own. He would understand she had taken the tough hand she was dealt and done her best.

My brother is built like the father he barely knew and moves like him, gracefully for a strongly built man—as if, as he goes about his business, he might break into a waltz. There are other similarities too. For my father in the good times the sky was the limit. Jeff's response when you wonder if some mad family occasion or travel arrangement is possible is always, "Everything is possible."

THE POSSIBILITIES SEEM LIMITLESS from the rooftop garden of Linda's apartment building on Manhattan's East Side. It's a warm summer evening. We've picked up salads at the Italian restaurant where my cousin is a regular, grabbed a bottle of wine, and settled in to contemplate the East River and the Queensboro Bridge. "Over the great bridge, with the sunlight through the girders making a constant flicker upon the moving cars, with the city rising up across the river in white heaps and sugar lumps"—for Nick Carraway in *The Great Gatsby* the bridge was built with the hope and money of the American dream. Uncle Sy, a boy from Praga, left Poland and lived the dream in his mansion in New Jersey. His business, Skyflite Luggage on Communipaw Avenue in Jersey City, was where my father went that last time to ask for money. Linda, who was there, remembers it. It took her a long time to tell me about it. "He took the money and he went away. It had to be before '67, so I would have been eighteen."

I want to know what she was told about my father's story. "They were in the cattle car from Warsaw going to Treblinka and somehow there was a window and he was small enough so they pushed him up," she says. "He lived in a cave kind of situation where he couldn't stand up." The box under the ground.

Her father said little about what had happened in Poland. "I heard he had tried to get his mother out of the ghetto. He had money then, and influence. He spoke to somebody who contacted her but she didn't want to leave her six other children."

Sy had not been an easy father. "You saw *The Pianist*, right? It changed my life. When I saw that movie all the anger I felt for my father was totally washed away. I can't blame him for being angry and drinking. Who wouldn't want to drink and forget?"

Linda remembered our family's implosion. "I believe your mother contacted my parents because she was distraught. Instead of being in the store your dad would be out feeding the birds.

"But of course your father was so damaged. I think your mother tried for a long time. I don't think she just bailed."

I ask Linda whether Sy and my father got on. "That's a good question. I don't know whether they loved each other but my dad felt a responsibility to take care of him."

It occurs to me how heavy that duty was. Linda also remembers phone calls from Paul as he became ill. "I used to shake; he was just terrifying. He and your father were of course driven by demons."

Joe helped Linda to understand, just as he helped me. "Dear Joe convinced me to accept my Dad. I had hated him for a long time because he was an alcoholic and he was abusive and driven. But if I knew that my family went into an oven, were incinerated, I think it would be a little hard to sleep."

A few years before her father died, Linda proposed a trip. "I said, 'Oh, let's go back to Warsaw. Will you take me?'" Her voice drops into the guttural timbre of Wichtel implacability: "'No. No.' He never would talk about it. He never wanted to go back. That was gone."

Linda was with her father when he was dying. I envy her that. But she is able to see a positive side to my father's story. "If he was found dead on the street that would have been very hard. That's not what happened. He was found, he was rescued, he was treated, he was buried in a grave with a marker." I still struggle to see those positives but it's a comfort to be with my cousins. We share so much history and they knew my father, although the longer this search goes on the more I suspect that no one really knew my father.

MANHATTAN MUST BE WHAT the lyricist of *America the Beautiful* was thinking of when she wrote, "Thine alabaster cities gleam / Undimmed by human tears." Here it still feels safe to be Jewish. The ferry to Jerry's home in New Jersey takes us close to the Statue of Liberty. "Mother of Exiles," the poet Emma Lazarus called her. We rush out on the deck to take blurred photographs. But despotism is in the air. Just before we arrive in New York in June 2015, Donald Trump has announced his run at the presidency, promising to "make America great again". One of his platforms is to cut back on the number of refugees and immigrants allowed in, but it's the welcome and promise Liberty represented to my family and millions of others that made America great in the first place.

Jerry and Jill's house, sprawling and low slung, is in Tony Soprano territory. We spend the day by the pool with their dogs, eating, swimming and talking. "I know that when my dad found out his brother was alive he was euphoric," Jerry says. "Anything he could do, he would do. He had money and was more than willing to shell it out. But there must have been tremendous resentment on Ben's part. He probably thought, 'This guy didn't go into the camps. He got here and survived. He made all his money. I got nothing.'" Jerry understood from what he was told that my father was mentally unwell from his experiences. "Well, okay, I would be pretty crazy, too, if I lived underground for years."

Of course Sy had guilt. "Listen, he survived and almost everybody was dead. On top of this he felt rejected because his mother wouldn't come to the US. That rejection may have been what triggered his lifelong insecurity.

"My father was very concerned about appearances. He wanted to create the impression we were Camelot, like the Kennedys. For a few years I had every toy you could imagine. I had an electric car that I used to drive around wearing a little hat and a camelhair coat."

Linda had related a story her father would tell them about Poland. "He was maybe twelve, riding horses with his father. Troops were coming, I don't know which, and they had to run into the woods on their horses and hide because the soldiers would kill the Jews." Jerry also recalled this story. If Sy was twelve, the year would have been around 1920. My father would have been nine or ten. He and Sy had learned as little boys that there was always hiding in the woods, always someone after Jews, always someone out to get them.

"My dad was Jekyll and Hyde," Jerry tells me. "Early on he would be affable for a while, and then those affable periods got shorter and shorter."

Joe believed Sy was a kind and generous man. "I never saw that guy," Jerry says, "any more than I saw the guy who walked into hospitals and gave away everything in his pockets. That guy was long gone. If I ever argued my Dad said, 'There's only room for one man in this house. Get out.' I spent a lot of time out."

Sy gave Jerry a car for his seventeenth birthday but demanded the keys back every time they fought. Jerry was lifting weights in the basement with a friend one night. "Dad came down drunk and said to my friend 'Get out.' I lost it and told him he should go fuck himself. There was a quarry near our house and I was going to go to the edge and jump off. Show him. A little voice said, 'Yeah, but you'll be dead, so maybe you shouldn't do that.'"

Jerry took the next bus out of town with five dollars in his pocket and hung out with a tomato picker he met at a flophouse. Eventually he made his way back home. "When I got back, nothing from my father. It was like it never happened."

Like Sy, my father liked to put on the Ritz, although there were few opportunities. And the brothers were alike in other ways. Both spoke multiple languages. Both expected their children to achieve: my father took me to the library when I was twelve and tried to make me read Dickens; Sy drilled Jerry in maths, and played mathematical games with him. Both loved opera. "My dad would go to the opera and cry," Jerry tells me. Perhaps their adored mother had loved music.

My father told the doctors at Brockville that his business went on the rocks when shopping centres started selling suits off the rack. Sy had got into the same sort of trouble. He had made a lot of money during the war. "He had a gigantic factory with about a zillion sewing machines. The army requisitioned them and he had to go to work making uniforms and parachutes," Jerry tells me. But in the '60s he started losing money because luggage could be made more cheaply in places like Indonesia. "In 1966, when I was at college, he told me I had to come back and live in New York and go to New York University and help run the factory. You could see it just going down. It became harder and harder for him to keep up appearances. Part of that was 'I've got to give money to my brother' and that became impossible because he didn't have the money. But it's not like my father would ever say, 'That Ben, he's a pain in the ass.' We didn't have those kinds of conversations."

Jerry and a friend, a fellow economics student, proposed a rescue plan. "My father took one look at it and said, 'When you've been in this business as long as I have then you can tell me what to do.'"

Wichtel men weren't good at taking advice. "Yeah, he didn't have the ability to say, 'That was a mistake.' In my experience, if you want to have a long career and stay in business you have to be able to go, almost on a daily basis, 'Oops that was a bad idea.' Your father couldn't do it either."

By 1972 Sy was bankrupt. The factory was sold at auction.

Eventually, Jerry got some affirmation from his father. "We talked about his taxes over lunch in a restaurant somewhere off Broadway. It was the first time he ever acknowledged I could do something he couldn't. I was well into my twenties by then.

"And when he was dying he said to me, 'Maybe I wasn't such a good father after all. I could have done better.' A couple of years later it dawned on me I had got fucked again. He got to die peacefully, knowing he had made his peace with me. Okay, so I had this good five minutes. And the other thirty years, what about them? But then again I got to see my father as he died and you didn't get to see yours and that's something."

We talk about how fallout from the past has threatened Wichtel family ties. When Linda invited us all to her daughter's bat mitzvah, she shook off some of that legacy. Jill says Jerry was sceptical at first. "He said, 'Are you crazy? What do you think is going to happen with this?' But then it was not what we thought it was going to be and you were all there."

I envy Jerry and Linda their clarity, their ability to talk about everything with unflinching honesty. Jerry has stared down tough situations. There were the struggles with drugs and alcohol, but these are now decades in the past. When we meet he has recovered from major surgery. Given months to live in 2011, he had sought out a different doctor and lived for months near Cleveland Clinic, where he got a liver transplant and another shot at life. "All I wanted was a pitch to swing at," he says. He took a gamble. He jumped. He survived.

PLACES WHERE I NOW KNOW MY FATHER LIVED:

Warsaw, the place where he was born and grew up and which he saw destroyed.

Żelechów, the town near the place where he hid.

Stockholm, where he and Paul were sent after the war.

New York, where he was reunited with Sy.

Montreal, where he first landed in Canada.

Vancouver, where he courted my mother and worked at English Textiles.

Montreal again, from where he tried to come to New Zealand. Toronto, where apparently he worked at Gabrielle Motors. Brockville, where, apart from three months in Embrun, he was an involuntary patient at the psychiatric hospital until he died.

Over the decades of searching for my father we have visited all these places, several more than once, except for Sweden. There seemed little point. All I knew was that, like many survivors, he and Paul had spent time there. Some Swedes were in sympathy with Hitler. Sweden's sales of iron ore contributed to the German war effort. German troops and weapons were allowed to cross the country to occupied Norway. But Sweden also took in 900 Norwegian Jews and offered asylum to 8,000 Danish Jews. Raoul Wallenberg, the Swedish diplomat who disappeared at the end of the war while a prisoner of the Russians, managed to save up to 100,000 Hungarian Jews.

After the war, Sweden accepted survivors for care and rehabilitation. "The Swedish residents of the city would crowd beside the gate and give us food and clothes, anything they thought might make us happy," recalled an Auschwitz survivor sent to Malmö by the Red Cross. Perhaps there was a degree of remorse.

I check lists online of Polish Jewish refugees who found "safe haven" in Sweden after the war. There is no sign of Paul or my father. Another steer from my brother-in-law Jim sends me to the archive of the Jewish Community in Stockholm in the Swedish National Archives. When I open the PDFs the archives send there is a photo of Paul from his Polish passport. He looks healthy and elegant. The file for my father is much thinner. No passport, no photo, just some documents in German, English and Swedish.

Paul's file shows that he was using the Polish version of his surname and that in late 1947 the Hebrew Immigrant Aid Society in Sweden was in correspondence with the Jewish Immigrant Aid Society in

Montreal to help arrange his immigration to Canada. "We wish to advise you that Mr Janiszewski has a small manufacture of hand-bags and portfolios here in Sweden and would be able to take the whole workshop with the machines along with him to Canada. Besides he has got ... $3000 at his disposal." Like Sy, Paul is a maker of bags, although on a smaller scale. Joe told me that in Sweden he gave Dad a job.

Paul marries his second wife, Lillian, in Sweden and they have to reapply to immigrate as a married couple. They receive affidavits in support from Sabina and Sy. At some point Paul decides to go to the United States instead. "American Consulate decided to grant the Janiszewskis a visa on the basis of a sister's affidavit," reads the document. His occupation is listed as "workshop manager".

My father's file reveals that he too changed his mind, but in the opposite direction. He arrives in Stockholm by plane on February 6, 1946. He is now thirty-five. He is listed as "Jude", his occupation "Fabricator von stoff"—manufacturer of fabric. Within a few weeks he is living in a guesthouse, the Fredrikshef Pensionatet, at Styrmansgaten 4.

He applies first to go to the United States. In a letter in October to the Swedish Aliens Commission, signed in his beautiful Polish calligraphy, he states he has telephoned the American Legation, who "as yet ... have no communication from Washington, but directly they hear they will telephone me. All formalities concerning my Visa, journey etc are completed."

From February 1947 he is a textile worker at a factory at Fridhemagatan 42, operated by a Victor Eriksen. He is paid ten krona, just under three US dollars a day. By August 26 his plans have changed. In a faint handwritten note at the bottom of another form the word "Canada" can be seen twice. In March he had sought permission to travel from Sweden to Copenhagen "to see friends". There is a photo of him sitting smiling in an open boat beside a pretty young woman.

Perhaps she was emigrating to Canada. Perhaps she was the woman Joe said he had met in a displaced persons' camp.

Paul's file offers another of those fragments that generate more questions than answers: a letter from Estelle, who is living in Brooklyn. "Dearest Uncle Paul," she writes, "it is with a heart full of sadness that I am writing to you. Your life has been with so much trouble and upheaval that the thought hurts." She is writing on behalf of her mother, Sabina, Paul's sister. "As you know … Mom depends on myself, Jack and Joe for some money each week. However she feels she would even live in Canada and make a place for you."

My father leaves Sweden for New York in September 1947. Eleven months later Paul is still in Sweden and planning to go to Canada. He may be in touch with my father, who is by then in Vancouver, with a wife and his first child on the way. Meanwhile Estelle is encouraging Paul to come to the US. "Because of the war situation, business is booming," she assures him. "I have a great deal of faith in you because I know you are an intellectual man with good common business sense."

Then Estelle's letter strikes a perplexing note. "For the first time in my life Abe Wichtel and I have drifted apart in our friendship. He always liked me, but now he and I do not agree." I know from Joe that Sy and Joe's sister Estelle were close, and would meet for lunch and tête-à-têtes at a restaurant in Central Park. "I told him that I would do all to bring you here," Estelle writes. "He answered, 'Go ahead, but don't bother me. I won't help.'"

This is odd: we know from Paul's account of his wartime experiences that Sy made contact with him as soon as he knew he'd survived. And Paul's file suggests Sy had already provided an affidavit for him. "Don't let that bother you," Estelle continues. "I am sure you will have success wherever you go. In fact, I fervently hope that you will someday soon prove to Abe Wichtel that he was wrong." Paul and Lillian sail to the United States on the SS *Gripsholm* and arrive in 1951.

Something seems to have happened to sour the relationship between the two branches of the family, although it's clear the ties were never entirely broken since Paul and Lillian attended Jerry's bar mitzvah, and when Sy was dying Linda took him to Far Rockaway to see Sabina, with whom he had once been so close.

WE UNDERSTAND MORE OF THE TIMELINE that brought my father to Canada when, after years of frustrating searches, we finally get his immigration papers in 2017. They show he arrived in New York from Sweden on American Airlines on October 6, 1947, three years after being liberated by the Red Army in the vicinity of Lublin, about 170 kilometres south-east of Warsaw. A month later he left New York and drove or was driven, possibly by Sy, to Canada. He crossed the border at Lacolle in Quebec with a temporary visa and travelled on to Montreal. Three months later he was in Vancouver. Another month later, March 1948, he seems to have gained permanent residency as a landed immigrant under the Canadian government's "displaced persons initiatives", a policy of allowing entry to various European displaced persons.

By September 1948 he has married my mother. She is pregnant: just under eight months later my sister is born. Making up for lost time. In 1952 he is applying for Canadian citizenship. In the photo that accompanies the application he looks relaxed and elegant in his English Textiles and a jaunty bow tie. By April 1954 he is a Canadian citizen.

ON OUR LAST DAY IN NEW YORK we go to look at the annual Pride Parade before heading to the airport to catch our flight to Berlin. Two thousand and fifteen is no ordinary year. The Supreme Court has legalised same-sex marriage. Rainbow flags and balloons decorate shops. Throngs of triumphant people greet each other with "Happy Pride!" and "It's a great day to be alive." It is.

It is not, though, a great day to try to get to JFK airport. We abandon our gridlocked taxi and join a crowd of panicked people pulling suitcases, who can see Penn Station but can't cross Fifth Avenue to get to it. Eventually a policeman helps us across. We miss our connection to the Airtrain and finally make it to the airport ten minutes before our flight closes. After a breathless check-in we make for the bar. The bartender takes an age to concoct our two Bloody Marys. Each has salt around the rim, a small organic garden of vegetable matter, and a row of olives on a stick. He sees us looking doubtfully at his magnum opus. "It's on the house!" he declares, and brings us a couple of vodka shots for good measure.

We toast the crazy cocktail, the roaring, honking, gridlocked eternal pride parade that is New York City, and pour ourselves on to the plane back to Europe, the Old World.

CHAPTER 18

Rooted in this soil

The survival of 1,000 Jews in the area where Jews were massacred in the hundreds of thousands is an act surpassing human understanding.
Jewish Telegraphic Agency Daily News Bulletin, August 31, 1944

IT HAD BEEN A PLEASANT enough trip until then, watching from the window of our packed compartment on the Berlin–Warszawa Express as the scenery morphed from manicured German vistas to the more shambolic Polish countryside. We'd popped along to the dining car for żurek, sour rye soup, and Żywiec beer, our traditional kick in the guts to remind ourselves we are in Poland. Afterwards I went to find the bathroom. The entrance to the carriage was jammed with people trying to connect to the erratic wi-fi. Among things I now know about Poland: never carry your backpack in front of you on a crowded train. You won't see the small stairwell to the carriage exit before your foot disappears down it. I was flung backwards, hard against the door. If it hadn't been properly shut I might have added to the black comedy that sometimes accompanied our brand of tourism by flying from a moving train in Poland.

A young man grabbed my arm, but not before my right knee twisted at a sickening angle. It announced with an agonising stab that putting any weight on it was not a plan.

"Knee," I hissed at Chris when I managed to hop and drag myself back to the carriage. "Bad."

He flinched. We'd been here before. There was the time I had to be forklifted on to a plane in Queenstown after a family skiing trip. The doctor's racy account of my accident—"This lady, who is a journalist from Auckland, was skiing in a lesson at Cardrona when a snowboarder flashed in front of her and distracted her"—caused such hilarity it ended up pinned to the staff noticeboard at the Wanaka medical centre. Then there was the monster haematoma acquired in Akaroa when, sitting blamelessly on a stationary horse, I was kicked in the leg by another.

Our few days in Poland would involve wandering the streets of Warsaw searching out old addresses and trekking through cemeteries gone feral with neglect. We were stuffed.

In Warsaw a bemused porter helped Chris heave me off the train. We lurched into a pharmacy. None of the staff spoke English. I stared helplessly at a stand of support bandages. A beautiful young fellow customer in a hijab who could speak English took pity on me, gently negotiating with a surly pharmacist to sort out a bandage and a truckload of painkillers. Warszawa: place of the kindness of strangers.

At our little attic hotel in Chmielna Street, more kindness. Our host rushed to fetch his anti-inflammatory gel and ice packs. Chris prepared to call our insurers and arrange an early flight home. Give it a night, I said. By morning the knee took a little weight, although I moved with the grace and pace of a geriatric gastropod. The psychic pain I feel when in Poland now made flesh, I hobbled on.

Luckily, the first day involved mostly sitting down. We visited the Emanuel Ringelblum Jewish Historical Institute. Emanuel Ringelblum was a mild-mannered historian and activist who fought to stay alive in the Warsaw Ghetto, or, if not, to preserve the truth of what happened there. He was the founder of the Oneg Shabbat

Archives, a collection of clandestine documents—diaries, photographs, monographs, underground newspapers—written by valiant people in extremis and hidden in cupboards, milk cans, the ground. It includes Ringelblum's own journal, originally published in 1952 in Yiddish, and in 1958 in English as *Notes from the Warsaw Ghetto*.

Ringelblum escaped to the Aryan sector of Warsaw shortly before the uprising but was betrayed by a Pole. The Gestapo shot him, his wife Yehudit and their twelve-year-old son Uri in Pawiak Prison on March 7, 1944.

An Oneg Shabbat poster reads: "He who fights for life has a chance of being saved: He who rules out resistance from the start is already lost, doomed to a degrading death in the suffocation machine at Treblinka … We, too, are deserving of life! You merely must know how to fight for it!"

The archive contains the last requests of people going to their deaths: "I only wish to be remembered," writes educator Israel Lichtenstein. "I wish my wife to be remembered, Gele Sekstein. … I wish my little daughter to be remembered. Margalit is 20 months old today. She has fully mastered the Yiddish language and speaks it perfectly … She too deserves to be remembered."

Krystyna Duszniak, a Melbourne historian who specialises in researching Polish Jewish families and whose knowledge has proved invaluable, has put us in touch with Anna Przybyszewska Drozd, a genealogy expert at the institute. Anna has turned up some treasures. Before our trip, the arrival in my inbox of the registration cards of Paul and my father had had me letting out a spontaneous shriek of triumph, then tears: these were the sort of documents I thought were lost forever.

Anna tells us the cards began as a grassroots initiative. "There are little groups of people who come out of some kind of hiding. They heard, oh, there are some Jewish people in Lublin, let's go," she says.

Local committees took names and sent the lists on to the Central Committee of Polish Jews. The names had to be written on the back of any old documents that could be found. There was no paper left in Warsaw.

I have been able to make out some of the information on my father's card. In 1939 he lived at 34 Chłodna Street and 9 Miła Street. In 1942 his address is simply "Ghetto". Krystyna had already translated the next passage: "After the ghetto, he hid as a Jew in the Garwolin County," she said, "which makes sense in the light of what he told you."

Partisans and those who escaped ghettos and trains hid in the forests in that area. Among those found near where my father was liberated were survivors from the Majdanek camp on the outskirts of Lublin.

A Jewish Telegraphic Agency correspondent, in a bulletin filed from Lublin on August 30, 1944, reported: "German prisoners of war and officers associated with [Majdanek] camp told the correspondents that hundreds of children were among the exterminated victims. One of them testified that he was in charge of shipping to the German State Bank all the gold, jewellery, rings, watches and other valuables of which the victims were stripped. ... It must be remembered that survival of Jews in Poland under the Nazis is in itself a miracle. The survival of 1,000 Jews in the area where Jews were massacred in the hundreds of thousands is an act surpassing human understanding."

The correspondents were not just reporting, they were also helping survivors, compiling lists designed to put them in touch with relatives in the United States and Palestine. It was such a document I had been given in 2010 at the International Tracing Service in Bad Arolsen, listing my father among the survivors and Sy as his relative in New York.

An act surpassing understanding. Help to survive was sometimes available to those who had managed to escape. Emanuel Ringelblum wrote of hide-outs dispersed through the forest, Polish families providing food in return for payment. "In these cases, the partisans also protected the Jews in hiding from blackmailers and informers who might try to hand them over to the Germans."

Others joined partisan groups to fight. The chapter on Żelechów in *Pinkas Hakehillot Polin—Encyclopaedia of Jewish Communities, Poland—* refers to a Jewish partisan unit commanded by a Samuel Olshak in the forest nearby: "Several young people who fled the ghetto when it was liquidated, or who had managed to jump from the trains during the deportation to Treblinka, found their way to that unit." One may have been my father.

Some Jewish partisans joined up with communist units. Others were killed by anti-Semitic Polish partisan units or by the Germans— including, in 1944, Olshak. For a Jew in the forest, enemies could come from anywhere. The Jewish partisans used the Hebrew greeting "Amcha" as code when they met a stranger. It means "your people, your nation". A reply from a stranger of "Amcha" vastly improved your chances of living.

All we know for sure is that my father was in this area. We know he was liberated there by the Red Army in late July 1944, one of those whose survival was reported in the JTA bulletin as miraculous. There was anti-Semitism in the ranks of Soviet partisans but the arrival of the Red Army helped save my father's life.

Paul's registration card included the names of his parents, my Jonisz great-grandparents: Chaim Jakob (known as Yankel) and Brandla Frydman. It confirmed the address of the apartment where Paul lived with his wife Barbara before they were herded into the ghetto and Barbara was shot in the street: Flat 19, 29A Wilcza Street. Unlike my father's card, Paul's didn't mention his time in the ghetto.

Anna deduced that by 1933 my grandmother Rozalia had moved back to the nine-room family apartment at 2 Wrzesińska Street in the Praga district; Sy gave this as her address in his passenger manifest when he went to New York that year. She must have moved there to be with her parents after my grandfather Jacob Joseph Wichtel died—my father said of cancer; others were told tuberculosis—in 1928.

AFTER THE GERMANS there were few Jews left in Warsaw. My father told me he went back to see if anyone else had survived. We know from his registration card that he stayed in Flat 5, 263 Growchowska Street, Praga. What hope and dread must have been in his heart. Information about the fate of a family wouldn't have been easy to discover. Anna said in most cases people learned that everyone had been killed. "But then we have these miracles. Because we see Benjamin jumped." Benjamin jumped. It is only when Anna says this that it occurs to me other members of our family on the train may have tried to jump too.

During our conversation we traverse some of those still raw sensitivities. We discuss the use of term "Polish death camps", which is bitterly resented by Poles, with some justification. When the Germans and their then Soviet allies invaded in 1939, the eastern Polish territories became western Soviet republics and the western territories part of the Reich. Central Poland became a "General Government" ruled by the Germans. The death camps were German camps in occupied Poland.

She says she's angered, too, by the idea she hears sometimes in her work that all Poles were murderers. When I say that my Great-aunt Sabina got out before the war she corrects me. "No, not 'got out'. 'Emigrated' please." She doesn't like the implication there was a need for Jewish Poles to 'get out' in 1933, before Hitler set his sights on Poland. "Every little sentence and word is creating another reality." But in fact there was anti-Semitism in Poland in the pre-war era, in every era.

We mention the Jewish revival which, as we found in Kraków in 2010, was taking place in the absence of actual Jews. "More and more people in Poland accept their Jewish roots. Some of them dream about it," Anna says. "People admire the Jewish culture somehow because it's also the bridge to the past, which was killed during the communist time. Jews were killed in Poland, yes. But also Polish culture was killed in Poland." It sounds a little like convict chic in Australia: some of those who might once have disliked Jews now wish to be one.

Museums also create a reality. Since we were last in Warsaw, POLIN Museum of the History of Polish Jews has opened near the monument to the ghetto heroes where we wandered on our last trip. The museum's address is 6 Mordechaja Anielewicza Street, named for Mordecai Anielewicz, the "Little Angel" who died in the bunker at partisan headquarters, Miła 18, where we paid our respects at a memorial stone that rests on the rubble.

My father's registration card shows that between 1939 and 1942 he lived first twenty minutes' walk from here at Chłodna 34, then five minutes' away at Miła 8. By the autumn of 1942 he was still clinging to life in the ghetto, one of those described by Emanuel Ringelblum as "the dead on furlough". We don't know what date he and the rest of the family were put on the train or trains to Treblinka. Sometime in 1942 is most likely, although my father talked about snow, so it could have been as late as January 1943.

The museum is a defiant structure of concrete, glass fins and copper mesh by Finnish architects Rainer Mahlamäki and Ilmari Lahdelma. The entrance leads into a cavernous void. Many architects of Holocaust-related buildings reach for the void. An undulating wall represents the parting of the Red Sea: divine deliverance from slavery; the help that never came.

We go downstairs to experience a subterranean story of the Jews of Poland, a "directed maze" through time, told artfully with a lot of high tech. It's a moving story and the building is breathtaking but it feels a little empty. It's one of those museums that displays mostly reproductions, with few actual artefacts to provide a dialogue between the living present and the relics of the past. But maybe hidden below ground and empty is the perfect metaphor for how history worked out for the Jews in Poland.

At the museum I am privileged to see a face and hear a story from wartime Warsaw. Poland supplied the Reich with plenty of enthusiastic local helpers in its task of making the country Judenrein, free of Jews, but it also had the highest number of any country of people who, at risk of summary execution of their entire family, helped save Jews, those whom the state of Israel would later call Righteous Among the Nations.

The museum's resource centre arranges for me to meet Witold Lisowski. Witek, as he is known, kisses my hand in the courtly manner of a Polish gentleman. We sit smiling at each other for a while, waiting for our guide Krzysztof, known to us as Krys, to come and translate. After Krys relays the bleak essentials of my father's story, Witek says something to me in Polish. Krys translates: "He says the drama of your father's later life is rooted in this soil." Tears already and we've just begun.

Witek's family also lived in Praga. We have something else in common: Witek too lost his father when he was young. He was killed fighting the Germans. With war still raging, his mother travelled 100 kilometres to find his grave, buy his body from German soldiers, and bring him home.

Praga in those days was forty-two percent Jewish. The Lisowskis were close to their Jewish neighbours, the Inwentarz family. Witek, eight when the war started, was a friend of Josef Inwentarz, known as Dudek, who was a couple of years older. With the German occupation, the local Jewish families were imprisoned in the Ludwisin Ghetto and left to starve. Witek's older brother Janek used to sneak into the ghetto to take their friends what he could. Witek found out about this only after the war. "My brother was afraid to tell about it to us, to mother, because she would be angry. It was too dangerous."

When the ghetto was liquidated, Dudek's mother arranged for him to stay with a Polish family but the sons in the household threatened to turn him in. He worked for a while in the countryside but, fearing betrayal, ran away again and hid in the woods for as long as he could, surviving by eating food left in troughs for horses and pigs.

Winter was coming. A young boy on his own, near death, he risked seeking out a friend. "I was just getting back from Scouts and he came out from behind a jasmine bush and called to me," Witek says. "Although we had spent all our childhood playing in the same sandpit I didn't recognise him. When I got just one metre from him he falls down. I took him in my arms and brought him home. He was very, very starved so he was light and it was not a big deal to carry him."

Witek's mother got the older boys to burn Dudek's vermin-infested clothes. Semi-conscious, he was put in a bath. "My mother held him with one hand and with the other hand she washed him, and she kept crying, telling him the words I will never forget: 'Dudek, Dudek, my children and I already have losses in this war. Forgive us, we will give you whatever we have but we can't keep you here in our home.'

"Then my brother said, as if to himself, 'If our father had been alive, Dudek would have stayed with us.' Mother looked into my eyes and at my oldest brother and she said, 'Do you think the same?' We said we did. And she said, 'Well, Dudek stays with us.'"

These two Polish men who have never met before, Witek and the translator Krys, are weeping together.

The Lisowski house was busy, with a shop at street level. Dudek, hidden upstairs, was unable to go outside or even move during the day. Eventually, he was smuggled out of Praga to an aunt who was hiding with farmers. There he worked in the fields with the cows and lay low. Before he left he begged Witek to give him his birth certificate as proof he wasn't Jewish. "He promised me when he is caught by

Germans he will eat it." So for several months Dudek became Witold Lisowski. "Tac." Witek smiles. "Yes."

This arrangement put Witek and his family in mortal danger. Jewish boys could be easily identified, and Dudek was nearly caught once when he declined to strip and swim with his fellow cowherds.

Dudek's sister Rachela was sent to live with nuns but she couldn't bear to be separated from her mother and returned. Both she and her mother were murdered at Treblinka.

Dudek survived and emigrated to Israel. For some years he lost touch with the Lisowskis: relations were not good between Israel and Poland. Witek went on to become director of the Museum of the Polish Army, and it was here he met some people who knew Dudek. The two friends arranged to meet again and Dudek brought a group of young Israelis on a trip to Warsaw. Witek went to meet the plane. "All the youth, when they got off the jumbo jet they encircled me on the tarmac," he tells us. Dudek had told them the story.

Dudek wanted to meet old Polish friends but as a Jew he was unsure of his welcome. Witek organised some surprise visits. Dudek was greeted like a brother. "They cry on each other," Krys translates. Later Witek, a Roman Catholic, visited Dudek in Israel. "My brothers have passed away," Witek says softly. "Dudek was my brother."

Witek tells us little about his own family's suffering in the war except what happened near the end. "They say there are no miracles but try to imagine the house where we lived, which was Dudek's shelter—two or three months later in the Warsaw Uprising the house was completely gone."

The whole city was on fire. The Russians had already liberated the east side of the river Vistula, where Dudek and my father were. On the west side the Germans were still in charge. All Poles were marched out under SS escort. Paul, still trying to pass for Aryan, was among them.

"We believed they would kill us," Witek says. "Then we heard a big noise, louder, louder. We could still see in the distance the fire of our house. We all thought the end of world was coming." What they were hearing were a hundred Allied bombers. "The SS were afraid of those bombers and ran away." The Lisowskis took their chance, ran for the forest and were eventually liberated.

Witek, a former air force man, has something else to add. Krys struggles as he translates: "Among those flying crews there were New Zealanders," he says. "Many died on our soil." For a few moments none of us can carry on.

Thanks to Witek, Anna, Krys and the woman in the hijab, by the time we meet Krys again next morning in the café of our hotel there has been a thawing in my relations with this soil. We've had breakfast and are ready to go. The first stop is Warsaw University. My father told the people at Brockville that he did a year there, studying business. Perhaps he didn't carry on because, even before Hitler, restrictions were being placed on Jews in academic institutions. We find a file for a Bronisław Wichtel, a sweet-faced young scholar in round glasses, but this is not my father. He could be a relative, maybe a nephew.

Next stop is the Jewish Cemetery in Okopowa Street, used by better-off Jews since the late eighteenth century. It contains an estimated 250,000 graves, though only about a third of the headstones remain. I thought I was prepared for this visit but I find, as always in Poland, that I'm prepared for nothing. I have brought with me photos of our family headstones, numbered, from a website, but the place is vast and in the heat of summer like a jungle. Over decades of neglect, nature has brought riotous life to this place of the dead. We have had to spray ourselves for ticks.

Fortunately Krys has rung ahead and made an appointment with the director, Przemysław Szpilman. After the war, with most documentation in Warsaw destroyed, huge efforts began to index graves.

The Jewish Cemetery in Okopowa Street, Warsaw, 2015.

When he became director in 2003, Szpilman set to work cleaning up areas of the cemetery and creating an online database. He is related, he says, to Władysław Szpilman, the Polish musician whose account of his survival as a Jew in Warsaw became a book, and then the film *The Pianist.*

In yarmulke, overalls and gumboots, Szpilman looks like a sort of Jewish lumberjack and sets a cracking pace, leading Chris down paths, then plunging into the undergrowth. Krys walks with me as I hobble along and we're soon completely lost. Eventually we hear yoo-hooing and fight our way through a tangle of vegetation to a headstone we could never have located by ourselves. It is a double stone for my great-grandfather, Chaim Dov Wichtel, and my grandfather, Jacob Joseph Wichtel. I find myself taking the headstone in an atavistic embrace, pressing my cheek to the sun-warmed stone. I'm in the

Double gravestone for Chaim Dov Wichtel and his son Jacob Joseph Wichtel, Jewish Cemetery, Okopowa Street, Warsaw, 2015.

stream of history. "Take a picture!" Krys tells Chris, but the moment has passed. I'm back in 2016 and self-conscious.

We move on to the small headstone of my great-grandmother, Brandla Jonisz, who starved to death in the ghetto. The date is August 29, 1941. How could she, a prisoner of the ghetto, have been buried here in 1941? Szpilman says that early on Jewish families could pay to bring their dead out of the ghetto for burial and attend their funeral. The Nazis were still trying to maintain the fiction that those imprisoned were in the hands of normal human beings and living some sort of normal life.

We pause to pay our respects at the site of a mass grave of prisoners of the Warsaw Ghetto near the cemetery entrance. In the archives of the United States Holocaust Memorial Museum there are photographs of the filling of mass graves here. In 1941 a German army sergeant,

Heinrich Joest, decided to take his Rolleiflex and record what was happening to people in the ghetto. The photos were discovered by a journalist in the 1980s. Bodies lie at the bottom of a pit. A young Jewish boy pauses in his work of dragging bodies to the pit to have his photo taken. Joest's caption on another photo reads: "Between all of the bodies of adults thrown into the grave, lay also [that of] a small dead child."

Some of my family may be in this grave. Not everyone managed to live, or wanted to live, to make it on to the train to Treblinka.

There is also a statue that can be viewed only through tears. In *The Pianist*, Władysław Szpilman writes of happening upon the very scene that it depicts: doctor and writer Janusz Korczak and the orphans he cared for being led by an SS man to the Umschlagplatz to board a train to Treblinka. A twelve-year-old is playing his violin. The little ones are singing. Kosczak, who was given the opportunity to save himself but refused, is carrying the smallest. "I am sure that even in the gas chamber, as Zyklon B gas was stifling childish throats and striking terror instead of hope into the orphans' hearts," Szpilman writes, "the Old Doctor must have whispered with one last effort, 'It's all right, children, it will be all right.'"

I struggle to find words for the charged atmosphere in places like this. "My heart felt heavy and full at the same time," my daughter Monika will say when she goes to this cemetery the following year. Her boyfriend Sean managed to capture in his photographs the haunted, clamouring silence. "The atmosphere of that place was transcendental," he said, "probably the only time I have found that word appropriate."

For the rest of the day we carry on, looking at as many of the addresses as we can. In some places the old buildings are long gone. Miła 8, at the epicentre of the uprising, was bombed or burned to the ground. Was my father taken from there to the Umschlagplatz?

Chłodna 34 may not be the actual building that was there before the war, but in this place my father walked and lived in fear for his life. Janusz Korczak and his orphans were just across the road at Chłodna 33.

Before December 1941 part of Chłodna Street was in the ghetto. After that the road separated the "big ghetto", with the poorest people, from the "little ghetto", where the intelligentsia and the better-off lived and the Judenrat was based. A wooden footbridge was built in early 1942 near Chłodna 23 and 26 to allow Jews to cross from one side to the other. It lasted only six months. As the ghetto was liquidated and its residents slaughtered, there was no need for so much space.

We stop for a beer at a café at Chłodna 34. Krys starts talking to a man who is there with his laptop, having a drink. It turns out he works on a website that shows how buildings lost in the war once looked. In Warsaw the past is never far away.

We wander along the road to an installation constructed in 2011 at the place where the bridge was. *A Footbridge of Memory* by architect Tomasz Lec consists of two poles with optical fibre strung between them. At night the fibre recreates the outline of the bridge in light. In windows in the poles there are images of ghetto life.

In Praga, where there was much less destruction, we find Wrzesińska 2, home of the Jonisz family. It was here that Yankel and Brandla brought up their ten children in a nine-room apartment, and here that my grandmother Rozalia returned as a widow. The place looks abandoned but there are satellite dishes. Someone lives here with our ghosts.

My father would have known this place as home. It's a large brick block, five storeys high, with small balconies. A lane with a vaulted ceiling runs through the middle. The door to the stairs is open so we sneak in. The place is in bad shape. In the lobby most of the old letterbox doors hang off their hinges. I remember that the family hid

The nine-room apartment in Wrzesińska Street, Praga, Warsaw, where Yankel and Brandla Jonisz brought up their ten children, and where Rozalia Wichtel returned as a widow.

some valuables—my father's ring and watch among them perhaps—in the basement, which Uncle Paul was able to retrieve and use to survive. When he arrived in America he still had a few small diamonds sewn into the hem of his coat.

I walk up the stairs thinking of the people who were driven from this house, then slaughtered. Molecules of desolation mix with dust motes in shafts of sunlight.

CHAPTER 19

Żelechów

Has delusions of persecution.
Dr V, Certificate of Renewal under the Mental Health Act,
Brockville, December 23, 1969

WHAT DO I NOW KNOW OF MY FATHER'S LIFE DURING THE WAR?
He jumped from a train to Treblinka and rolled down a bank into snow.

He ran. (Sometimes, after the war, he still ran in his sleep.)

He ate eggs raw. He ate potatoes he dug up, along with the dirt.

He ate horse meat.

He ate anything he could find.

He saw many tragic things.

He saw a woman have her breasts shot off.

He and a companion met young German soldiers and tricked them by pretending to have pistols in their pockets. The soldiers brought them food.

He was in the underground resistance.

He hid in a box under the ground in the vicinity of Żelechów.

IN 2014, GOOGLING "WICHTEL" AND "HOLOCAUST", as I do a lot with the urgency of a strung-out addict seeking a hit, I'd found a new document on the United States Holocaust Memorial Museum website, a slightly different version of the registration card I already had from Anna. It recorded: Beniamin Wichtel. Date of birth: 1910. Father's name: Jakób. Mother's name: Rozalia. Place During War: Żelechów.

Krystyna Duszniak has described Żelechów to me as "a small village near Garwolin … a real pre-war shtetl [that] hasn't changed all that much today." We head there on our last day with Krys. He brings his friend Janek along for the hour-and-a half drive from Warsaw. Janek, a small humorous man in his early seventies, is an expert on Jewish cemeteries. "His nickname is indicative of the interests he indulges in," Krys says dryly. "Cemetery Hyena."

Janek speaks better English than he lets on, and his interests prove wide-ranging. When we get to Krys's car there's what I take to be a parking ticket under the wipers. In fact it's an advertisement for entertainment involving underclad ladies. With a serene smile and an air of scholarly interest, Janek tucks it into his folder. It takes me all day to figure out that he has no Jewish heritage because when we enter a ruined Jewish cemetery, he pulls out a carefully folded yarmulke. He tells me later he wears it out of respect for the dead.

Żelechów was a place of Jewish settlement from the early 1700s. At the beginning of the Second World War, seventy percent of the residents were Jewish. Now, as far as I know, Jewish population: none. Many Jews fled here from the advancing Nazis. When troops arrived on September 12, 1939, Jews were attacked in the streets and their property looted. Houses were torched, and on September 13 the synagogue burned.

This is the territory where Samuel Olshak's partisan unit operated. "Janek speculates that those who jumped off the train probably knew that in Żelechów there was a partisan group they could join without being afraid they were joining Polish partisans, who were quite often not friendly to Jews and even killed Jews themselves," Krys says.

Janek thinks my father and the man who escaped with him might have jumped near Małkinia, the last big transportation junction, where the engine was moved from the top of the train to the rear to go in the opposite direction, to Treblinka. "They probably jumped off not far from there because in those areas they were given some chance to survive—the train went into forest." My brother-in-law Jim has identified another possibility, the small village of Urle. This was another place where Jews jumped because it was surrounded by forest. My father could have made his way to the Żelechów area from there.

There were more jumpers than anyone thought. A German historian, Tanja von Fransecky, in her study *Jewish Escapes from Deportation Trains*, identified at least 764. The Jewish activist Leo Bretholz described using a urine-soaked sweater to bend the bars on the window of the cattle car he was in. It could be done.

The book *The Warsaw Ghetto: A Guide to the Perished City* has accounts of jumpers taken from the archives of Israel's World Holocaust Remembrance Centre, Yad Vashem. "The boldest went first, mainly young boys who had no one from their families with them," reads one account. Others were presented with a dreadful choice. "Those who felt they would still be able to jump but could not part with their nearest and dearest were particularly distressed."

Jumpers were sometimes encouraged. Joe said my father had talked of others helping to push him out the window. But some faced bitter reproach from those they were about to leave behind. My father may have faced just such an agonising dilemma. When I asked that question "How could you leave your mother on the train?" he had not answered.

IF WE'D COME TO ŻELECHÓW a few years earlier we would have seen more of the small wooden shtetl houses where the Jewish inhabitants lived. A few remain but a renewal has been going on. The rynek—town square—one of the largest in Europe, still has its original undulating cobbled surface, over which we bucket as it makes alarming contact with the undercarriage of Krys's car.

Janek speaks of a man he knows, a survivor from a similar village. When the man returned to his home after the war he asked about his sister, who had been hidden with some local Poles. He learned she had been given away to the Germans by someone who had claimed to be a saviour. "How could a person start living again next to such betrayers?" Janek says.

We go to the Jewish cemetery. Just a few headstones are left, enclosed by a wire fence to keep the ghosts in or the vandals and anti-Semites out. To me these empty silent wild places speak louder than the grandest monument about what happened to the Jews. As usual there is no official sign or memorial, just a notice put there by a Jewish organisation. "On September 30, 1942, the Jews were deported to Treblinka … Over 300 of them they murdered later in the town and buried in this cemetery. Their memory is a blessing." Nearby are the ruins of a mikveh, a ritual bath. No sign there either. The only monument is to non-Jewish Polish heroes.

Grażyna Frankowska, a former teacher and principal of the local school, has lived in Żelechów all her life, and preserves the history of the town, including Jewish history, in a memorial chamber at the community centre. She lives not far from the centre of town in a modest house with her daughter's family. Krys and Janek greet her with kisses on the hand; Krys uses the formal honorific Pani Professor (Madam Professor). In the parlour, surrounded by files of photos and documents, we are offered cherry cordial in tea glasses, pound cake, and the district's spectacular strawberries.

Grażyna tells us, in unstoppable streams of sibilant sing-song Polish, that many of the cemetery's headstones were used during the war to pave a courtyard of the local police station. After the war the owner of the building said he would return the headstones to the cemetery.

Grażyna Frankowska, a former school principal who preserves the history, including Jewish history, of Żelechów, the town near which Ben Wichtel hid underground in a forest during the war.

He didn't keep his word. The stones ended up in a dump somewhere.

Grażyna was born during the war so she doesn't remember much first-hand, but her parents and other family members lived in this place and seventy percent of their friends and neighbours, the people whose shops they frequented, were led off and killed. I get Krys to ask Grażyna what the older generation might have said about what happened to their Jewish neighbours but my question seems to get lost in translation.

Eventually little stories are offered. She tells us her father hid two Jewish girls for two nights "in a barrel of small grains". Her father attacked a German officer who was beating a young man. "He smacked this German soldier in his face, even drawing out one of his teeth," Krys translates. "The German went crazy and my father quickly ran away and hid in our home. But Germans ran after him. They wanted to search our house, so my mum sat on the floor on the place where there was a trapdoor to the cellar where my father was hiding, and pretended to be sick. She told them she suffered from typhus. They were always in fear of typhus."

We don't talk about anti-Semitism in Poland today but it becomes clear not everyone appreciates Grażyna's inclusion of Jewish history in the local record. "Someone came with one old sneaker shoe and offered it to her. 'Look, Grazinka, this is a shoe some Jewish gentleman wore,'" Krys says. "It was to ridicule her. Peasant-minded people are not enough understanding."

Not enough understanding: no Jews came back here to live after the war, Grażyna says, but survivors and their children visit. "They want to see." She loads us down with publications about Żelechów and some traditional cut-paper patterns she makes in her spare time. We visit the memorial chamber she has created. It is full of artefacts of old Żelechów, and photographs of the synagogue, and of smiling Jewish girls at the local school before the war. When it's time to go we try to give her a koha, a contribution towards her work, but she won't hear of it. This is her gift to survivors, their children, the truth.

WE ARE TREKKING into the forest in Okrzei, less than half an hour from Żelechów, when the panic kicks in. Poland has begun to feel less like a charnel house, a place where my family's degenerate DNA was hunted, but here we are once again in that by now familiar locale the middle of nowhere, following three Polish men we scarcely know to the scene of another mass murder.

We are in the company of Urek, a local man who has kindly driven us, total strangers, from his farmhouse as far as his vehicle can go and is now walking with us into the forest. It's mid-summer. He lights a cigarette, smokes it down, and chucks the smouldering end into the brittle vegetation underfoot. He lights another. The forest looks tinder dry. We are going to die here.

This is near the end of a day that has got completely out of hand, even by our standards. After leaving Grażyna's house, Chris told Krys we'd like to see some forest if possible, so we can visualise the sort of place where my father might have hidden. Krys has taken up the challenge with gusto. We have documentation that my father was liberated in the Lublin area so he has made some calls and we have headed here, twenty-six kilometres south-west of Łuków.

There is no forest in sight. We stop at a wedding venue in the countryside. It is named Dwór Sienkiewicz after Okrzei's famous son Henryk Sienkiewicz, a writer and Nobel Laureate who in 1896 wrote the popular historical epic *Quo Vadis*. Later I will Google the book and find a description that says there is not a single friendly reference to the Jews anywhere in the novel. "What is worse, nearly every mention of them is tied to some ugly rumour or malicious deed." I am not surprised to read that Sienkiewicz "merely followed the received opinions of his day".

While Krys goes inside the venue to make enquiries, we sit in the car for what seems long enough for three Polish weddings. It's early evening already. We have to be up at three the next morning to fly to London.

"You'll have to tell him we need to go back to Warsaw," Chris says.

"I can't!" I wail.

Eventually we troop inside, where Krys has baled up the receptionist.

She's told him there is a memorial to murdered Jews in the forest but she doesn't know exactly where. These things are seldom signposted. Trapped behind her desk, she rolls her eyes as he makes her go through her contact book. Poles seem willing to engage in complicated interactions like this with strangers.

She makes a couple of calls, is at a loss. It seems hopeless. I take Krys aside and say we really need to get back. He turns and gives me a hard look. "Do you want to find it or don't you?" Resistance is futile. We will be late back to Warsaw that night.

The receptionist finally rings a schoolteacher, who proffers the name of a man on whose land the monument may be. The man's not home but his wife says he won't be long. To the relief of the receptionist, we turn and bolt out the door to drive to his farm.

IN THE FOREST THE ONLY SOUNDS are the calling of birds and the crunch of our footsteps. In a sunlit clearing there is a headstone organised by the Lasting Memory Foundation. It sits over an indentation in the ground. There is a hole made by an animal on one side. Perhaps a fox has made this place its home. This is where thirteen Jews died when Germans found their bunker and threw in grenades. A box underground: is this the sort of place where my father hid?

There are only three names on the stone: Chana Besser, Mosze Besser and Rywka Milbrot, women from nearby villages. The Lasting Memory Foundation lists among others murdered here two brothers, Maks and Sergej, from Żelechów, and two twelve-year-old boys, Moszek and Dawidek. The "ek" is an affectionate Polish diminutive: Little Dawid; Little Mosze.

On the day the stone was dedicated a doctor from Prague, name unknown, was also remembered. He had escaped from Treblinka after an uprising there in August 1943. Of the 300 prisoners who managed to get away, 200 were hunted down by German SS, police and military

Memorial stone erected at the site of an underground bunker by the Lasting Memory Foundation in the forest at Okrzei, near Żelechów. Here thirteen Jews in hiding were discovered and killed by German grenades.

units. The doctor saved a Jew from another group who were hiding nearby by amputating the man's severely injured hand. The patient was Wacław Iglicki, who had jumped from a train.

Iglicki had ended up in the forest with a partisan unit. His account, on the website of Centropa, a non-profit Jewish historical institute, offers some insight into what happened to people like my father. "Before we got to ... Siedlce, because that's more or less where I jumped out of the train, there were many dead people underneath me already ... My friend Mendel ... jumped out first, then I after him. But I didn't find him because the train was moving so I might have been a few kilometres away from him already. The direction I wanted to take was this: go towards my place of birth. So I walked towards Żelechów."

The crowded ghetto where you wake up and the person next to you is dead. The airless cattle car where you have to stand on the dead. The box in the ground where you can't lie down. From September 1939 until July 1944 my father fought to live in a world with literally no room for a Jew.

As Urek speaks the unresolved tensions of Poland's Holocaust history play out again. I wonder if his family knew at the time that Jews were hiding on their land. "He knows some stories," Krys says, "that his grandfather was ordered to deliver Germans to this area but nothing came out of it. Logically he's convinced they must have known, but he doesn't know the right story behind [the Germans] finding this place."

Urek was happy about the bunker monument but his encounter with the foundation hadn't gone well. The president was Zbigniew Nizinsky, a non-Jewish Pole dedicated to finding the unmarked graves of murdered Jews and Poles. It seems Urek was told that when the Germans came to the site of the bunker their pathfinder was a Pole.

Telling the story, Urek fires off a burst of angry Polish. Krys translates. "He questioned: Did this man, the pathfinder, have a name written on his forehead?" The question of who might have led the Nazis to the bunker hangs in the air.

When I return home I read online a story of a similar bunker in Okrzei on the land of a farmer. The farmer knew he was hiding Jews. His son led the Germans to the place and they killed them all.

Nizinsky visited many families in Okrzei to try and find the location of bunkers like this. "Nobody knew. Nobody could locate the place." Nobody knew: the silence in Poland can be deafening. "It took Mr

Nizinsky several visits and he finally got to me and I was able to take him here," Urek says.

"Nie, nie nie," he says when Janek asks if the site was ever excavated. Excavation was not unusual. People would come with metal detectors, looking for guns or gold. But according to Urek the bodies of the people murdered here—the Czech doctor, Moszek, Dawidek and the others—remain undisturbed. The Foundation for Lasting Memory reports on the ceremony that was held to dedicate the stone to them: "The rabbi and the priest prayed together, breaking the utter silence of the forest."

Urek tells Krys he's heard the bunker actually hid fifteen Jews. Two escaped the grenades. This is enough to convince Krys that my father could have been one of the fifteen. "You know what? Maybe it happened that he went to arrange for provisions when the attack took place and that's what saved him."

"Imagination," Janek says quietly, with a wink.

"I know," I say. But I'd love to believe it. All I know is what those who met him when he came back from the war said: that he had lived in a forest in a box under the ground. "The ceiling was low, so that once inside one couldn't stand up," one survivor of life in a bunker recalled. "The roof was made of wood, covered with branches and sand. We also had a stove made of bricks, and a concealed door..."

When Dad once made us a play house it had walls, a door and a window, but disappointingly no roof. That was so it didn't kill the grass, he said. Maybe he didn't want us to even play at living in a box. In *Fugitives of the Forest*, the author Allan Levine records a scene witnessed by Jewish partisans coming out of the Rudniki Forest in Lithuania behind the Red Army. A woman who had been hiding in a small cave in the ruins of the Vilna Ghetto emerged with her young daughter in her arms. The child, who had been quiet, finally spoke. "May one cry now, Mother?" she said.

I hug Krys and tell him he was right to push the woman at the wedding venue for information, right to get us to this powerful uneasy place. In my search for my father, I tell him, I sometimes haven't pushed hard enough. "You have to put aside your sensitivity when it comes to extending a little bit of push," Krys advises. I promise to extend more push.

Urek has another story. In one corner of the bunker, he says, there was a tree with a Star of David on the trunk. He cut it down two or three years before the monument was unveiled. "Why?" I ask Krys. "Because it was completely dried out," he translates. "It was a strange tree. It was of solid size but after the war it didn't develop. It kept drying, drying, drying until it finally died." Maybe it was just a coincidence that the tree refused to grow, Krys explains, "but Urek saw this Star of David with his own eyes."

We stand staring at the indentation in the ground, a home to some animal, a mass grave. There's a point in *The Pianist* when the building in which Władysław Szpilman is hiding catches fire. To go out is to be caught and sent to Treblinka. Szpilman decides to take an overdose of sleeping pills so he won't be conscious when he burns. Somehow he wakes up still alive and feels not disappointment but joy, a "boundless, animal lust for life at any price".

My father must have felt like that when he jumped and didn't get shot, when he could emerge from his bunker in broad daylight, when he could breathe free again. Perhaps that's why he came to his Aunt Sabina's in Brooklyn smiling, with his guitar, full of life.

PART IV

CHAPTER 20

A mitzvah

Family and friends present at the burial: none.

Brockville, November 30, 1970

WE DECIDE WE PROBABLY WON'T say Kaddish, the mourner's prayer. My cousin Linda has suggested it, and its ancient Aramaic cadences sound beautiful: *Yit'gadal v'yit'kadash sh'mei raba/ b'al'ma di v'ra khir'utei…* But there is the translation: "Glorified and sanctified be God's great name throughout the world / which He has created according to His will." My father didn't believe in any of that.

First things first: more phone calls at dawn, asking questions you could not have anticipated ever having to ask, such as whether it is possible to replace a grim, wrongly spelled pauper's plaque in a Catholic cemetery in Ontario with something more… Jewish?

Dale Trickey thinks that will be fine. We can have a small upright headstone. On top of the cost of the stone, there's a small fee for the City of Brockville and an even smaller one for the St Francis Xavier Cemetery. When I ask him to recommend someone in Brockville to organise the stone, Dale seems reluctant. It turns out there are two options. One of the companies is run by Tammie Trickey but he is hesitant to recommend his wife.

I fire off an email to Tammie. It's the beginning of a correspondence marked by a singular sunniness, given the subject matter. "All is good on this end. Stone has been ordered. Hope you had a wonderful Valentine's Day!" And, when the time comes to send drawings of the finished design, "Sorry, I thought I attached the corrected version," she writes. "Lol I see I did not. I have now!"

We need some lols. The wording on the headstone has presented challenges. Group emails fly between my brother, my sister, me and our children. The third generation, relatively free from all the unpacked baggage of the second, and fierce champions of the grandfather they never knew, make sure we get it right. Something in Hebrew, says Nicola. A Star of David, says everyone.

Chris points out we should have proper dates, not just 1910–1970. My father's birthday: May 16, the same as my sister. The day he died: November 26, four days before he was buried on my birthday.

Should we say "Loved husband of Patricia"? They were never, in the end, divorced. "You know your Mum and I … don't wish to hurt anyone," Stew had written from Japan. My mother had told me, in tears, that she had never stopped loving my father. She makes it on to the stone. Not in a shack on Milford Beach but in a cemetery in Brockville, Dad has finally pulled us all together again.

I want to mention on the headstone that he was in the Warsaw Ghetto and survived the Holocaust. Jeff says there should be some indication he had a life after that.

There are two choices of size. "The taller one leaves room for more great-grandchildren, which is good. No pressure, cousins and siblings," writes my son Ben, who has produced three.

We agree all my father's descendants must be listed. I ask my stepson Ben if he would like to be included. "I would be honoured," he says. Twelve and counting. Sometimes just a list of names can feel like a victory.

The design we're sent looks fine except for two small but crucial spelling mistakes: "granfather" and "Holcaust". I begin to appreciate the terrible potential for cock-ups implicit in the expression "set in stone".

I confess to a Jewish friend that I have become obsessed with this quest, these journeys, this headstone, all too late. "Don't sell it short," he says. "You are all doing a mitzvah."

So we are doing a good deed. The unveiling is planned for June 19, 2016. Not everyone can make the trip, including our sons Ben and Ben, my sister's son Karl, and Nicola, who was with us when we found the grave in 2015. Cousin Joe is too ill to travel from Pennsylvania.

That still leaves thirteen. Jerry, Jill and the dogs will come up from New Jersey. Jerry will have competed in a five-kilometre race at the Transplant Games at Cleveland Clinic two days before. "It was eighty-five degrees, humid, with a twenty-miles-per-hour headwind," Jill emails after the race. He placed second in his age group.

Linda will come up from New York. Her daughter Mollie, who will be in New Zealand on a post-graduation visit, will travel with Ros, Chris and me from Auckland.

Jeff and his wife Maureen have just moved to Guelph, Ontario, where Jeff is dean of a large veterinary college. They have ended up in a new home only four hours' drive from our father's grave and have visited it again since we went for the first time in 2015. He saw so little of his father as a child. Now he is close. For the unveiling, he will pick up the New Zealand contingent from Toronto's Pearson Airport. His daughter Jocelyn and her boyfriend Blair will drive up from New York State, where Jocelyn's working as the newest vet in the family. Our daughter Monika and her boyfriend Sean will already have flown in from London. It's a transcontinental logistical nightmare. "Anything is possible," Jeff says.

We end up, many of us dazed and jetlagged, at the Super 8 Motel in Brockville. It's hot. There's a pool; water always helps. The headstone gathering is the following morning. There's a feeling of mounting pressure—some final reckoning approaching, like a rogue weather system. Chris thinks we should go to the cemetery and check that everything is in order with the headstone. No, no, I say. I can't bear to look. What if something has gone wrong? Something does go wrong. There's an argument in a liquor store with my sister. Long-simmering tensions erupt over the legacy of the past. I remember my father and Uncle Sy yelling in the library. I fear we have made a scene.

We go out to dinner. I resist a powerful urge to drink too much. This sort of thing can't be done hung over. It was never going to be easy. Through grappling with these tensions over the family history and dynamics I have learned that children in a family can have entirely different experiences. I have realised that not everything I thought I knew was true. There is always more than one story and I can only tell my version. You can search forever and never fully know what happened. The dead are entitled to keep their secrets.

Eva Hoffman, a psychologist and the child of survivors, in her book *After Such Knowledge* describes trauma as "suffering in excess of what the psyche can absorb". The pain is so intense it can arrest time, "freeze it at the moment of violence or threat … In a sense such memories are not memories at all, since their content has not been relegated to the past."

This helps explain why children of survivors experience our parents' stories, their memories, with such visceral immediacy. These are not memories in the normal sense but invitations into a still unreeling present. My father occasionally gave me a glimpse into a world so livid and clamouring that for years it made the one I inhabited seem unreal.

Austerlitz, the title character in W.G. Sebald's novel about memory and the Holocaust, is a small child when he is sent away on the Kindertransport to England. He grows up to forget his past, only to find the past won't forget him. "I feel more and more as if time did not exist at all," he says, "only various spaces interlocking according to the rules of a higher form of stereometry, between which the living and the dead can move back and forth as they like and the longer I think about it the more it seems to me that we who are still alive are unreal in the eyes of the dead."

I think about these things as three generations gather to commune with a past that suddenly feels more vivid and pressing than the present. I think about what my father, a person displaced, was going through in Brockville. Eva Hoffman has written: "Fury at having been persecuted may burst out suddenly in behaviour that strikes others as perplexing or unwarranted."

From some voyages there is no return. In my father's years at the Psych the past finally outran him. He was back in the ghetto, back in the forest. He sometimes thought we had been sent to safety with his brother, who would care for us and educate us. At other times he believed his brother's wife was spying on him, out to destroy him, because clearly someone was. "He stated he was frightened and persecuted all his life," his doctors wrote. They put it down to psychosis.

IT'S JUNE IN BROCKVILLE. The young cousins from all over and their partners are happy to be together, a rare event. They play with the dogs, drink beer, take photographs to post on Facebook and Instagram. There is also an invasion of the absurd. At the eleventh hour, an email arrives from Tammie: "Hi Diane, Dale just popped over to the Cemetery Plot and noticed the bag was off. He did put another one back on. I am sorry the only thing I could find was a plastic bag." She adds a sad face emoticon. The covering we will remove with great solemnity from my father's headstone is a black rubbish bag. I think that would have made him laugh. Linda informs us it's Father's Day in Canada.

This time we have no trouble finding the spot. There's the rubbish bag. Tammie and Dale have, touchingly, added a festive ribbon. The day is warm and windy. The soundtrack is provided by birds, the odd car hooning up the cemetery drive, and Monika's Sean on guitar.

Jeff undoes the ribbon. Ros and I pull off the rubbish bag. The headstone looks solid, enduring, like the memorial shards dedicated to unnamed murdered Jews we saw all over Europe. This stone will leave no one in any doubt about who, however improbably, is buried here.

Sean plays Elvis's "Love Me Tender", the only pop song my father admitted to loving, and *Du, Du Liegst Mir Im Herzen*: *"You, you are in my heart / You, you are in my mind."* My brother speaks first. "We need to acknowledge all the difficult journeys we've had both physically and spiritually to get us all here today. In our own ways we have all tried to honour the memory of Benjamin Hersz Wichtel, but our inability to be with him in his final years when he needed us most is a heavy scar on our hearts."

I say a few words about the search that got us here, the generosity and honesty of those here and those who couldn't make it, in offering support and sharing painful memories. One of the hardest things to read in my father's file was the account of his funeral in 1970. "Family and friends: none." Now look.

Jerry speaks of two brothers: "When Ben came to my bar mitzvah, he brought a million ties. When I went to a bar mitzvah, I brought a suitcase," he says. "We grew up in a house of smoke and mirrors. My father was omnipotent ... We were told he was surprised and thrilled that Ben had survived ... Ben was presented to us as financially irresponsible, demanding, and unable to manage a business. The unfortunate irony is that was true of both brothers."

He speaks of meeting my father only twice in all those years, at the bar mitzvah and when he came knocking at the door, alone, one night. "We were all children. We had no power or control over any of it. Now we, the living, have come together, hoping to find some closure and some peace."

*Wichtel family and partners dedicate the headstone for Ben Wichtel, St Francis
Xavier Cemetery, Brockville, Ontario. Left to right: Ros Bartleet, Jill Wichtel,
Mollie Wichtel, Jerry Wichtel, Linda Wichtel, Diana Wichtel, Chris Barton, Sean
Fleet, Monika Barton, Jeff Wichtel, Blair Ellis, Maureen Wichtel, Jocelyn Wichtel,
June 19, 2016.*

Tears are shed. My daughter, who can cry at the sight of an old
man out walking his sausage dog, is our official weeper for the day. She
has lived through the hopeful highs and crashing lows of the search,
never mind the epigenetic legacy. "I bullied Mum, I downright bullied
her because I couldn't believe that we didn't know," she says. "It was
heartbreaking for her and all of his children, and then for the next
generation who wanted to know where our granddad was.

"I've got to thank all his kids for never giving up, and I'm not
sorry for bullying you, because we are here. And Ben, Granddad, I
don't really know what to call you but I'm so glad we are here. You
are a hero in my eyes. I'm sure there must have been times in your
life when you felt like you failed but you didn't. We're here to assure

you of that. Not only did you not fail but you triumphed and we will never stop telling your story."

My sister-in-law Maureen reads a message from Nicola to her grandfather: "I wanted to take a moment to let you know how proud I am to be a Wichtel. To hold the name of a man who lost everything to the wars of other men; the name of a man who fought so valiantly for survival in the most dismal of circumstances; the name of a man who brought my father and beautiful aunties into this world; the name of a man who taught me just how unfair life can be, and to never take for granted the people you love. ... You have, and always will be, a strong presence in my life. May you sleep soundly once and for all."

Never forget you are a Wichtel, my sister and I were told in the middle of the night nearly half a century ago.

My sister Ros speaks of loss and compassion. As Sean plays "Oh My Papa", the song our father loved to hear his daughters sing, we place stones on his headstone.

Blair and Jeff's daughter Jocelyn makes sure these unorthodox proceedings are recorded. The partners Chris, Maureen, Jill, Sean and Blair step in to take care of one or the other of us in the moments when things get messy. As I write, eighteen months later, I've only just felt able to look at the recording for the first time.

Later my daughter will do did what her generation does so naturally: put it all out there. She posts a photo of the headstone on Facebook. "Last year my family found my long-lost grandfather's grave after half a century of searching. Today I finally stood in front of it for the first time and we unveiled a beautiful new headstone with all our names on it so he wouldn't have to be alone anymore."

The names: Loved father of Rosalind, Diana and Jeffrey. Honoured grandfather of Karl, Benjamin, Benjamin, Monika, Jocelyn, Nicola and great-grandfather of Sam, Ruby, Ari.

Headstone for Ben Wichtel, St Francis Xavier Cemetery, Brockville, Ontario, June 19, 2016.

The words we put together: "Benjamin Hersz Wichtel, May 16, 1910 – November 26, 1970. Holocaust survivor, survivor of the Warsaw Ghetto, fighter in the forests of the old world who started again in the new."

NEARLY HALF A CENTURY TOO LATE, it's done. There's a lunch in Brockville, where I feel giddy with release of tension. We say goodbye to the dear American cousins. We will see Linda soon when we go to Pennsylvania to visit Joe. Meanwhile the rest of us will go to Ottawa, where it turns out that an afternoon at a vast crazy waterpark near Cornwall—where my father was picked up—is not a bad way of dealing with being intermittently ambushed by grief. We stay a few nights at Jeff and Maureen's new home in Guelph, where my father's misspelt grave marker from the Psych rests under a tree in the garden. The first spring it was there Jeff took a photo of daffodils growing where it lay. They were not planted, he said, nor were they growing there the year before.

After Monika and Sean head back to London, Jeff, Maureen, Ros, Chris and I hit the road for Allentown, Pennsylvania. There's a palaver at the border as we are ordered out of the minivan so border control can pay unnerving attention to our clutch of New Zealand passports. The variety of roadkill we encounter driving south is arresting: deer, a porcupine, and a sight that's hauntingly sad and, say the Americans, rare: a young bear, the pale soft pads of its paws turned upwards to the sky.

In Allentown we have lunch with Joe, Barbara—"My adorable wife," Joe calls her—their daughter Elyse and her family. Joe, now eighty-six, is more frail than when we saw him last and relies on an oxygen supply, but his spirit and humour are unvanquished. "Why didn't we know each other earlier?" he says.

In 2011, the last time Chris, Jeff and I visited, we attended a ceremony where Joe received a Human Relations Award from the City of Allentown for his work as a Holocaust educator at local colleges. "You can't tell the Hitler story enough," he tells me. "Young people find it unbelievable because it is unbelievable—the best Germans devising the best method of conducting mass murder and the

Joe Lubell, who never stopped fighting against forgetting, Allentown, Pennsylvania.

participation of ordinary Germans, Ukrainians, Hungarians, volunteers to kill the Yid."

At the ceremony, attempts to wind up Joe's speech as he set about laying into the Republicans had proved futile. Our cousin has conducted an implacable war against cultural and historical amnesia and all manner of bullshit. He's only recently retired from his work because of his health. Over lunch there's a lively discussion of the political situation. Some like Hillary Clinton, some prefer Bernie Sanders. Of course none of us believe that Donald Trump will be elected.

Before we leave, Linda tells Joe how much his wisdom and understanding have meant to her, that he changed her life. I've told him this too. There's still much to be understood and relationships to be healed, but the mitzvah that Joe has helped make happen has been done.

On January 30, 2017, seven months after our visit, I hear from Elyse that Joe has died. I never get the chance to tell him there has finally been contact with the family of our other cousin Dora, the one who survived the war in Poland with the papers of her Catholic school friend's dead sister. Two years after I posted a message on a likely-looking Facebook page, Dora's grandson Nir Herszenborn, who lives in Guadalajara, Mexico, finds it. He sends a text. Minutes later we're talking face-to-face online.

Nir knows the basics of Dora's story but little more. When he was ten, his teacher suggested to the children in his class that they ask their grandparents about their wartime experiences. He rushed home and asked his grandmother. She burst into tears.

Although he's been to Poland, Nir didn't manage to find the family graves or the house in Praga. I send him photos. A short while later he puts me in touch with his father Felipe, one of Dora's two sons. Felipe tells me that in the ghetto Dora's mother Dina was forced to make a devastating decision. "My grandmother had to choose which of her two daughters would be able to survive better outside the ghetto. Since my mother was the oldest she was chosen. They bribed the guards at the gates and so she was able to escape." She lived. Her parents and sister died at Treblinka.

Felipe's father, Israel Herszenborn, was also in the Warsaw Ghetto. "He survived exactly the same way as your father. He escaped from the ghetto and survived as a warrior in the wilderness."

When the war ended, Dora was working as a maid for a Communist politician, Władysław Gomułka, on an estate near a village in Poland. There was a parade. Israel was with the Russian Army, marching under the Star of David as part of a group of Jewish fighters. "My mother was very excited to see Jewish fighters so she went up and kissed my

At Yad Vashem, Israel's Holocaust memorial museum, a cattle wagon used by the Nazis to transport Jews to death camps has become a Memorial to the Deportees. During the mass deportations from Warsaw to Treblinka of 1942–43, up to 100 people were crammed into each wagon. Ben Wichtel jumped from a window like this.

father. He said, 'Well she's a very nice-looking girl so I think I will stay with her.' They stayed together for fifty-two years."

Felipe and I, newfound cousins, children of survivors, smile at each other via our online video chat. This is a happy family story to share. I tell him I wish we'd known each other earlier. He says, "I think it's a very great blessing to meet in this time."

It is. After Dora died her two sons lost contact with their Jonisz family. Now more pieces of the family puzzle have found each other in cyberspace. Joe would have been happy about that. I'd spoken to him on the phone about a week before he died. We didn't talk much about the past.

"How's the writing going?" he'd asked.

"You're an important part of the story, Joe," I told him.

"I know," he said.

DANIEL MENDELSOHN TOLD ME what he wanted to avoid when he wrote *The Lost*. "I've read a number of Holocaust non-fiction books where they skate, I think, dangerously close to 'What I got out of the Holocaust'." He's right. There's no personal growth to be had in that fathomless void.

I'll hang on to the guilt. Along with love, it's all I have to offer my father. In this sort of story it's the ones who don't feel any guilt you need to watch out for.

People say, "Well, you must have got some closure." There's no closure. It's better to stay in the stream of history. That's where he is. It's where he's always been.

"WHO IS THAT, DI-NANA?" Sam is six and has noticed for the first time the photograph on the chest of drawers in our bedroom. "That's your great-grandfather, my father," I say. "He's your dad's grandfather Benjamin. Your dad is named after him."

"Is he dead?"

"Yes, he died a long time ago."

"What happened to him?"

I open my mouth to speak, close it again and change the subject. Who could put that horror and tragedy into the head of a sweet funny six-year-old?

Later I tell my daughter-in-law Carolyn I'm not sure what to tell him, or when. She reminds me there's another story I could tell, just as my father told us stories about stealing eggs and pretending to have guns and tricking young German soldiers in the woods.

"Polish Jews had three options," Matthew Brzezinski writes in his book *Isaac's Army*, an account of resistance and survival in occupied Poland. "They could run. They could hide. Or they could take up arms and fight. The only other alternative—to do nothing—resulted in almost certain death."

Death also found most of those who ran, hid and fought, but many, even young children on their own, did it anyway. "They refused to submit to evil, or to give up on life, and this made them exceptional individuals—not just as Jews or Poles, but as humans," Brzezinski writes. "Statistically they were the 'one percent', the very few who took their fate into their own hands and beat the odds."

There is the unbearable narrative I have lived with: my father was hunted and imprisoned; almost everyone he loved was humiliated, starved, beaten, stripped, robbed, murdered; everything and everyone he had was taken from him, twice; he went crazy.

But there's never only one story. My father was a badass. He fought for life. After the ghetto, after the train to Treblinka, he still managed to work, play his balalaika, sing, click his heels and fall in love. He survived to help others when he could, to make a family that goes on. Benjamin jumped. Next time Sam asks, I will tell him the story.

ACKNOWLEDGEMENTS

Many thanks to Mary Varnham of Awa Press, who rang one day and said, "You have an unusual family background. Would you like to write about it?" To Jane Parkin, who provided another pair of eyes on the manuscript. And to designer Keely O'Shannessy.

I am grateful to the Grimshaw Sargeson Fellowship for four magical months of writing on the edge of Albert Park in the company of birds and my ghosts; to Bauer Media and the *New Zealand Listener* for readily allowing me time off to write; and to Steve Braunias, for encouraging my first tentative attempts at this story. Special thanks to Brian Boyd for support and encouragement from the start, and to Finlay Macdonald for his expert advice and acute perspective.

Thanks to the Archives of Ontario; Citizenship and Immigration Canada; the Swedish National Archives; POLIN Museum of the History of Polish Jews in Warsaw; United States Holocaust Memorial Museum; Yad Vashem Holocaust Museum in Israel.

For help and kindness beyond the call of duty, I'm grateful to Kathrin Flor at the International Tracing Service in Bad Arolsen, Germany; Krystyna Duszniak of *Lost Histories* in Melbourne; Anna Przybyszewska Drozd of the Emanuel Ringelblum Jewish Historical Institute in Warsaw; Krzysztof Malczewski, our indefatigable guide in Poland; Przemysław Szpilman of the Jewish Cemetery in Warsaw; Grażyna Frankowska in Żelechów; Witold Lisowski, who shared his family story; Claire Dionne at the Russell Branch—Township of Russell Public Library, Ontario; Dale and Tammie Trickey in Brockville, Ontario; Sandy and Margo Thomson in Vancouver; in Montreal, Alan Greenberg of the Jewish Genealogical Society and Janice Rosen of the Jewish Immigrant Aid Society.

Warmest thanks to friends made through the Auckland Second Generation Group, especially Deborah Knowles, Lilla Wald, Naomi Johnson and Sara Nevezie, and to Anne Hartwell, who provided renewed friendship, memories from Vancouver, and old letters.

This book is about family. To my father and mother, who told me what they could of what they went through, I owe everything. My deepest gratitude goes to my aunts Rosemary McKinstry and Wendy Perrier; my brother-in-law Jim Stevenson, who generously offered his invaluable research skills; my wonderful cousins Linda Wichtel and her daughter Mollie Wichtel; Jerry and Jill Wichtel for their memories and their courage; the late Joe Lubell, my dear friend, teacher and bridge to the past, who never stopped fighting against forgetting. His memory is a blessing. And to his wife Barbara and their family; my cousins in Mexico, Nir Herszenborn and his father Felipe Herszenborn, for sharing memories of Dora Jonisz. I'm deeply grateful to my sister Ros, with whom I have shared this history for so long; to my brother Jeff, who so wholeheartedly makes so much possible, and his wife Maureen; and to my fierce, amazing nephew and nieces: Karl Bartleet and his partner Jasmine Kim, Jocelyn Wichtel and her partner Blair Ellis, and Nicola Wichtel.

My deepest gratitude and love to my partner in everything, Chris Barton, for his support, intelligence and unflinching honesty. He has walked, laughed and cried with me every step of the way. Without him, nothing is possible. Finally, our children and their partners—Ben and Carolyn Alpers, Ben Barton, Monika Barton and Sean Fleet—have put up with a lot and responded by offering more love, support and inspiration that I could ever have hoped for. They and our grandchildren Sam, Ruby and Ari are the future my father never stopped trying to believe in.

ILLUSTRATION CREDITS

Cover: Ben Wichtel in Sweden sometime between February 6, 1946 and October 6, 1947: Wichtel Family Collection

PART I

PART II

PART III

PART IV

INDEX